Easy Walks in Monarch of the Glen Country: Badenoch and Strathspey

ERNEST CROSS

Luath Press Limited
EDINBURGH
www.luath.co.uk

First Published 2006

The paper used in this book is recyclable. It is made from low chlorine pulps produced in a low energy, low emission manner from renewable forests.

Whilst every effort is made to ensure that information in this book is correct, no responsibility can be accepted for any accident, loss or inconvenience arising.

Printed and bound by
Digisource GB Ltd., Livingston

Typeset in Sabon

Contents

Map Notes

THE SKETCH MAPS in this book are for walk planning purposes only. They are not a substitute for a proper map. The most widely used and available maps are those produced by the Ordnance Survey. For all practical purposes there are two kinds to choose from:

Landranger, produced with a scale of 1:50,000, which is about 1¼ inches to the mile,

and

Pathfinder, the Outdoor Leisure series, produced with a scale of 1:25,000, which is about 2½ inches to the mile. This series is very detailed, and shows every field boundary, fence and wall.

The following maps serve the area covered by this book:

Sheet 35 – Kingussie and Newtonmore, 1:50,000

Sheet 36 – Grantown and Cairngorm, 1:50,000

Aviemore and the Cairngorms, 1:25,000

Harvey's walkers maps cover the main Cairngorm mountain area.

National Grid references are used in walk descriptions.

The Visitors Guide to Rothiemurchus is a valuable aid for walks in that area. It is freely available at the Visitor Centre at Inverdruie, and at various other points in Rothiemurchus.

The Forestry Commission Wayfaring map provides unequalled detail for parts of the Queen's Forest.

Map Reading

You will find that OS map references are used and quoted here and there throughout the book. They are a great convenience, and save an enormous amount of positional description. Everyone should know how to read a map reference. For those who cannot, this is how it is done:

All OS maps are based on the National Grid. This is a system of imaginary 1km squares covering the entire

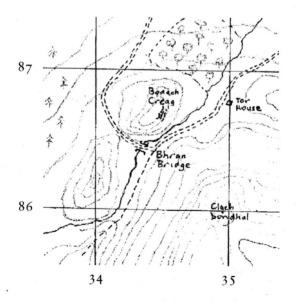

country. Each mapping area comprises a 100km square with a two-letter identifier. Each area has 100km sides.

The squares are aligned roughly N-S and E-W, and the 1km squares are numbered from the bottom left from 00 – 99 in each direction. When quoting references the E direction, to the nearest 1/10th, is always given first.

In this example, taken from 100km square AB, Bhran Bridge has the reference AB343864. It really is that simple. It is well worth a little effort to become familiar with the technique. Map reading ability increases the enjoyment of the countryside out of all proportion to the effort involved.

MAP KEY

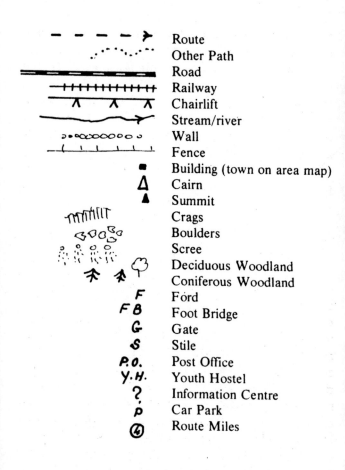

✈ - - - - →	Route
⋯⋯	Other Path
▬▬▬	Road
+++++++++	Railway
⋏ ⋏ ⋏	Chairlift
～～	Stream/river
∘•⫘⫘∘ ∘	Wall
⌐⌐⌐⌐	Fence
■	Building (town on area map)
Δ	Cairn
▲	Summit
⏛	Crags
⌬⌬⌬	Boulders
⁖⁖	Scree
🌳	Deciduous Woodland
🌲	Coniferous Woodland
F	Ford
F B	Foot Bridge
G	Gate
S	Stile
P.O.	Post Office
Y.H.	Youth Hostel
?	Information Centre
p	Car Park
④	Route Miles

Author's Note

THIS BOOK COMES towards the end of a very long love affair with the Scottish Highlands that had its beginnings in Argyll over 60 years ago. There is a song that some Liverpool football supporters sing with the refrain 'You'll never walk alone'. That could also apply to mountaineers, and I want to acknowledge the support over the years of Pat, who has put up with my many absences, and of Phil, Ben, June, Jane, Alf, Dave, and all the other countless friends and companions who have provided such delightful company down the years in the forests and hills of Strathspey.

The predecessor to this book, *Short Walks in the Cairngorms*, was written to satisfy a need for a guide book for people who did not want an extensive and exhausting day out in the mountains. Many thousands of copies were sold between the first publication and its demise following the closure of the chair lift which, over the years, had been used by many thousands of walkers as a means of quick and easy access to the mountains. The Cairngorm Mountain Company and Scottish Natural Heritage have specifically prohibited pedestrian access to and from the mountains from the funicular, so there is little in this book about walking on and about the main Cairngorm massif. Perhaps the earlier book relied too much on the sheer accessibility of Cairngorm at that time, even though there is a wealth of other walking country throughout the region.

This new publication has retained some popular and

easy excursions from the earlier book, and has added a number of new walks, but it still only scratches the surface of the walking possibilities in this uniquely beautiful National Park. The more energetic may wish to use the companion volume *Hill Walks in the Cairngorms*.

The verse of W H Auden's, appearing in Walk 18, is taken from 'O What Is That Sound?' and is reproduced from his *Collected Poems* by kind permission of Faber and Faber.

Ernest Cross
2006

Foreword

THE CAIRNGORMS AREA, as a whole, is being increasingly affected by the kind of recreational and economic pressures that have created so many problems in the National Parks of England and Wales – and we are all part of that problem. A Government-convened Working Party, chaired by Mr Magnus Magnusson, KBE, studied the problems and suggested various remedies, and a Cairngorms Board was established in 1994 with the job of overseeing the future development of the area and its transition into the Cairngorms National Park, which was established in 2003.

The new National Park has an area of more than 2,500 sq miles (>3,500 sq km) and is the largest in Britain. It is also proving to be quite controversial because the new authority does not have direct control of planning, unlike the situation at Loch Lomond and in all the other National Parks in England and Wales. This is a very valid criticism because there have been several questionable permitted developments in the area in recent years, of a type that would certainly have been rejected in the other National Parks. Some organisations think that the boundaries are too tightly drawn, and that the Park should have included, for example, the Angus Glens, Glen Tilt, and more of the Monadhliaths. All of which is now academic: the park exists and all concerned will have to learn to live with it and in it.

From the visitor's point of view very little will seem to have changed, and the main effects are as follows:

Priority is being given to the regeneration of the existing areas of Caledonian forest, and two new forests have been designated: Strathspey and Mar.

Where expedient, access may be controlled (this covers all land: mountain, moor and woodland).

The practical effects are very evident in and around the Queen's Forest in Glenmore, and in the other Forest Enterprise woodlands in the area. Rather than adopt a piecemeal approach to the forestry which could, for the time being, have left attractive stands of mature trees here and there, Forest Enterprise has engaged in a rigorous programme of wholesale clearance of all non-native trees and shrubs. It is a form of arboreal ethnic cleansing, which means an end to the serried ranks of Sitka spruce, Douglas fir, Lodgepole pine, larch, etc., and has created a tremendous mess in the affected woodlands.

When our grandchildren are very old there may be a new woodland of native trees throughout Strathspey. In the meantime we must put up with the devastated clearings and take comfort in the knowledge that it is all for the common good, and that time and nature are great healers. The cleared areas are already becoming quite attractive scrubland, but it is rather ironic and something of a black joke that the regeneration so far seems to consist of abundant seedlings of Sitka spruce and other alien conifers, and there is an almost total absence of seedling native trees. Is there a message here?

Apart from some new parking restrictions, the main impact on outdoor pursuits has been the expenditure of a great deal of public money on replacement of the Cairngorm chairlift with a new funicular railway. The rail track, which looks like something left over from the construction of a spaghetti junction on the motorways, is a concrete and steel structure that does nothing at all to enhance the landscape. The funicular is to provide better and easier access to the mountain for the dwindling numbers of skiers. Outwith the skiing season the funicular can be used only for an expensive visit to the 'Interpretation Area', café and shop below the summit, and the mountain is closed off at all times to pedestrian access to and from the funicular.

What a pity that the so-called conservationists did not go to Snowdon in Wales to see how the Victorians did things, or to Austria or some of the other Alpine regions to see how – with proper and enlightened management – walkers, skiers and other mountain users can all be accommodated with little or no damage to the environment, and without irksome and controversial restrictions.

Introduction

HUMANS HAVE ALWAYS walked, which is probably why they have legs; for most of human history people have walked from place to place simply because they have had to. Walking for leisure and pleasure are generally thought of as modern concepts, but they are not all that new, and there must always have been people who enjoyed walking for its own sake. Indeed, at the beginning of the 17th century Thomas Coryate walked to Venice on a sort of pedestrian precursor of the Grand Tour. His journey took him through much of Europe, and the resulting book, *Coryate's Crudities*, is an entertaining and, at times, hilarious story of his travels; it was published in 1608. Few books on the subject were published for many years after this, and walkers as a class were quite unpopular later in the 17th century. On the whole they were regarded as vagabonds, and they were treated, or maltreated, accordingly. It was not until the late 18th century, when people like Wordsworth, Coleridge, de Quincey and Southey discovered the English Lake District, that walking in the country purely for pleasure became a recognised leisure pursuit; for a long time only a fortunate few could enjoy it.

One of the problems, of course, was that until quite recently the majority of people had neither the time nor the means. There was an upsurge of hiking in the 1930s – the Ramblers Association dates from then – but the real explosion came only after the end of World War II. Less drudgery, more leisure and more money may be some of the most significant benefits of the new industrial revolution that came about during the last half of the 20th century. Whatever the reasons, more people than ever before now regularly enjoy the pleasures that can only be had from staring nature in the face whilst travelling on one's own two feet.

The countryside of Badenoch and Strathspey is an ideal place to do this, but it is quite untypical of the country elsewhere in Britain, and it would be extremely difficult to find another holiday area where all the trappings of modern life coexist so closely with areas of real wilderness. This is a big country, and everything is impressively large; the maps are notable for their lack of marked paths, and it is all rather different from much of the other countryside in Britain. The mountain areas are renowned for their remoteness, and the removal of the Cairngorm chairlift poses a major problem for hill walkers. Similar difficulties face low-level walkers also, and there may seem to be little scope other than the waymarked trails in the forests. But just like life itself, the appearances are often deceptive, and there are plenty of places to walk.

This book is about where to walk – it is not about how, or why. But there are some practical points, not at all obvious to the tyro, which might usefully be explained. Although many of them don't know it, most walkers are probably naturalists at heart, which means that they have an interest in natural things, but not necessarily a scientific interest. They just want to enjoy all that a walk can offer, including the wildlife, and the wildlife here is probably more varied than anywhere else in Britain. The following principles, once understood and then practised, can add greatly to the pleasures of any day in the country.

The vast majority of people see and hear little of the wildlife of the hills and woodlands, and most conclude that wildlife is scarce or extinct. It is not, and one's every step is carefully observed by it because most walkers telegraph their coming for many miles ahead. First, there is a matter of dress. It is popularly supposed that a red or orange anorak renders rescue more certain if one is lost or injured on the hill. This may be true, but brightly coloured clothing is easily seen by all the wild things, and they instantly go to ground or depart. The muted hues and soft shades of traditional tweeds and hunting tartans are not a sign of restraint – witness the splendour of the dress plaids – nor do they signify reckless tendencies on the part of deerstalkers, shepherds, and other working hillmen. They were a practical response to the need for unobtrusive dress by a people whose very livelihood was tied to a successful hunt or pillage. The principle remains, and brown, beige, and 'cow-pat' green are all good colours for the country. Tweeds are in vogue again, and the newly ubiquitous Barbour is a boon. Untreated quiet cottons, like Ventile cloth, are worn by many serious naturalists.

Other factors are noise and vibration. To see wildlife during a country walk it is necessary to be quiet, so tread lightly, walk softly, and refrain from chatter. Try to develop a 'third eye' which senses what is behind the next tree, and don't be in such a tearing hurry. The seasoned nature watcher tends to spend a lot of time loitering, apparently doing nothing much at all, but that extra hour on the walk can be quite exhausting as well as most rewarding: sustained concentration is hard work. Small groups are always preferable to large parties, and it is an advantage to be walking into the wind. All these factors add up to one thing: minimal disturbance to the natural inhabitants of the countryside. Please remember that it is their world as well as ours, and that they live here whilst we are merely visitors. It is really just a form of courtesy; try it, and be pleasantly surprised by the difference it will make.

One last point: in general, most of the routes can be reversed, and the differences in aspect are so great that this effectively doubles the number of walks.

Glenbogle and the Monarch of the Glen Country

WHEN SIR COMPTON Mackenzie wrote *Monarch of the Glen* in the mid-1930s he placed Glenbogle in a reasonably well-defined region between Lochaber and Badenoch, a little to the northeast of Spean Bridge, and somewhere not a million miles away from Loch Laggan. Ecosse Films, the company that created the modern TV series *Monarch of the Glen*, has adopted a more broad-brush approach to locations, facilitated by modern transport and much improved roads.

The TV programmes, although originally panned by the critics, have proved to be very popular with TV viewers in fifteen different countries worldwide. One result of this has been to open up to the general view of TV audiences a delightful area of Badenoch and Strathspey that extends from Ardverikie (Glenbogle House) in the south to Grantown-on-Spey in the north. The small towns and villages in between have both a wealth of interest and a wide variety of attractive and dramatic scenery all

Glenbogle Gatehouse

around, and they offer plenty of scope for a range of outdoor activities. They also have become newly popular attractions in their own right because of their association with the TV locations.

Nowadays, between May and September, the TV people seem to be everywhere. From the Falls of Pattack near Laggan, to Broomhill (Glenbogle) Station on the Strathspey railway near Nethybridge, there is a rash of yellow 'MOG' markers pointing to the current filming locations. The actors are frequently to be seen in and about Newtonmore and Kingussie, and the local post offices have advertisements seeking extras for the crowd scenes. So it is now possible to combine a holiday with five minutes of fame, and the opportunity to rub shoulders with the luvvies.

The area is rich in historical associations, too, and Ardverikie has the distinction of being the base for the young Queen Victoria's long Scottish holiday in 1847. She very much enjoyed her very first Highland games at Laggan, and was so captivated by the location and the scenery that she and Prince Albert are said to have contemplated buying Ardverikie for their own use. But she loathed the wet August weather and the midges – some things never change – and she and Prince Albert leased the Duke of Fife's property of Balmoral, with its drier climate. As everyone knows, this eventually became the site for their favourite home and holiday haunt in the Highlands.

Ardverikie was also popular with Sir Edwin Landseer, who was often a guest of the owner, his friend Lord Abercorn. It is Landseer who provides the real connection with the TV series, because his original painting of *The Monarch of the Glen* was executed as a mural on one of the starkly whitewashed walls of the dining room. This painting, and several others, were all destroyed when the house burnt down in 1873. It was later replaced by the present, much larger and grander, house, which represents the Victorian Scottish baronial style at its most flamboyant. The house is difficult to get to, and access is by boat across Loch Laggan from near Aberarder, or down the long private drive from Kinlochlaggan. **It is emphasised that Ardverikie is a private house and is not open to the public,** but there is a splendid view across the loch from a lay-by on the Spean Bridge road near Aberarder, and the gardens are usually open to the general public on one or two Sundays in the early summer in conjunction with the National Gardens scheme. Several of the smaller properties on the estate are let as holiday cottages through specialist agents.

FOLLOW THE COUNTRY CODE:

- Enjoy the countryside and respect its life and work
- Guard against all risk of fire
- Fasten all gates
- Keep your dogs under close control
- Keep to public paths across farmland
- Use gates and stiles to cross fences, hedges and walls
- Leave livestock, crops and machinery alone
- Take your litter away with you
- Help to keep all water clean
- Protect wildlife, plants and trees
- Take special care on country roads
- Make no unnecessary noise

CARE FOR SCOTLAND'S COUNTRYSIDE!

PART ONE

The River Spey

BADENOCH IS A land of many contrasts: its populous and fertile river valley is bounded by wild woodlands and rugged, untamed hills. To the west the Monadhliaths – the grey mountains – are a relatively trackless wilderness that is still largely unspoilt. To the east, beyond the Feshie, and dominating the finest remnants of the Great Wood of Caledon, the mighty Cairngorms rise in all their majesty. Technically a dissected plateau, they are the largest high landmass in Britain and an almost legendary area of sub-arctic tundra. They offer superb walking and climbing, and some of the best skiing in the realm. The glacial origin of the valley is quite clear, and the roads, rail and river keep close company as their route is punctuated by the succession of delightfully quiet and attractive small towns and villages that lie between Laggan and Grantown-on-Spey. From Newtonmore, the swift and sinuous ribbon of the Spey is the common thread that runs through the valley and unifies it all.

Rising in the remote and stony fastness of the Monadhliaths, some 3,000 feet up on the northern flanks of Creag Meagaidh, a little stream starts down towards the Corrieyairack Pass. The little stream is probably the real source of the river, although that honour is usually accorded to Loch Spey – further to the west and lower down, near to the watershed above Glen Roy. Some miles to the east, the impressive bulk of

Geal Charn dominates the north bank of Spey Dam. A rocky and lonely summit, it commands the bleak and windswept approaches to the Corrieyairick Pass. It also overlooks the lonely gathering grounds of two great rivers of the north. Beyond this mountain, in the remote and hidden fastness of the hills, innumerable burns run down to the northeast and then unite to become the scenic Findhorn. To the south, to the west and to the east, myriad springs and streams form a crazy network of watercourses that eventually come together in the Spey.

The country is wide and open here, and the mountains, though very high, seem very far away. There is no pretty scenery on these moors, but there is undeniable grandeur all around. It is all to do with scale, and the vast and empty spaces about the headwaters of the Spey emphasise the enormous size and sense of wilderness that are so characteristic of the Highland scene. The growing stream flows through wild hills and majestic landscapes, and through lonely moorlands where the only sounds are of running water, a curlew's cry, an eagle's bark, and the wind's mournful sigh. This is a lonely landscape at the best of times, and it underlines the puniness of man. On a wet and windy, and cold grey winter's day one can only marvel at the hardiness and fortitude of General Wade's soldiers, who built the Corrieyairick road through such a harsh and barren wilderness in 1731.

The infant river has many tributaries, and by the old Kingshouse of Garvamore Wade's magnificent twin-arched bridge crosses a sizeable stream. Spey Dam, near to Laggan, collects these headwaters into a pleasant artificial loch, and the flow is then controlled by the dam. There is never any lack of water here, and the river flowing under Laggan Bridge, only a few miles from the source, is a dark and swiftly flowing stream. From Laggan and on through Newtonmore, where there is a confluence with the Calder, the river is fairly well contained, but by Kingussie the country opens out and becomes almost gentle, and the ruins of Ruthven Barracks stand above a wide flood plain. The Truim and the Tromie boost the flow, and Loch Insh is actually just a widening of the stream. The Insh marshes are the largest area of fen and marshland in Scotland, and in winter, when the river is in spate, it is obvious why the region of Badenoch – the drowned lands – got its name.

The landscape here has changed again, and against the majestic backdrop of the Cairngorms and the Monadhliaths there is a sylvan wonderland of birch and pine woods, low hills, and willow scrub and alder carr. This is a staging point for an enormous number of wading birds and waterfowl, and an impressive range of species can be seen as they pass through on their migrations every year. The Feshie joins the stream beyond Kincraig, and from Aviemore the river runs dark and deep to the old ferry point of Boat of Garten, where it is now conveniently bridged. At the historic village of Nethybridge yet another confluence swells the stream, which flows on now through a pastoral and arboreal wonderland to a culmination at the important and delightful town of Grantown-on-Spey.

WALK 1

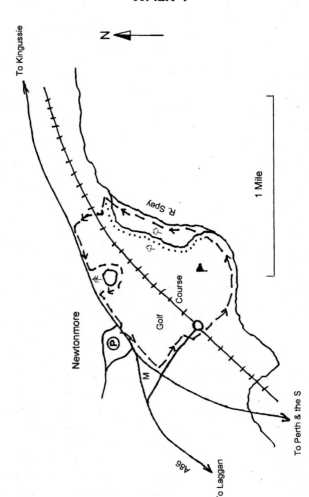

By the Bonny Banks of Spey

EAST OF LAGGAN the hills recede and Strathspey opens out into a broad, hill-girt river valley. This is very much a flood plain, and the river often overflows the banks in wet winters. The large area of water meadows on the left bank at Newtonmore is known as the Dale, and contains the golf course and grazing for the local crofts. This is a particularly interesting stretch of river, and the frequent changes in the flow during previous spates have left a long and sinuous island, *Eilean na Cluanaich* (the Island of the Pasture) which lies between two arms of the stream. The walk makes a delightful change, and presents about two miles of serene and varied riverside, a wealth of wild flowers, and masses of birds, some of which are rarities. The resident otters, being largely nocturnal, are unlikely to be seen.

Walk down the main street and bear left at the Laggan road junction. The Clan MacPherson Museum (Glenbogle Tea Rooms) is on the right. Entry is free, and it is well worth a visit. From the museum go left down Station Road, but just before the station, a finger post on the right indicates the field path, which should be followed across the railway track (do take great care while crossing this) and down to the river.

Go to the left, and stay close to the bank and walk over what is, effectively, the out-of-bounds rough at the edge of the golf course. Considering the nature of the land here, there is an amazing variety of plant life, and the water meadows are famous for their orchids. There is also a lot of stunted birch scrub and other woodland. It should be noted that this particular stretch of river is part of the Insh Marshes SSSI (Site of Special Scientific Interest) and the whole of the Spey from source to estuary is a EU SAC (Special Area of Conservation).

Decide whether or not to cross to the island, and continue following the river. The scenery is a delight, with the low hills on Nuide Moss in the foreground, backed by those outliers of the Cairngorms, the seemingly distant Glen Feshie hills, over to the east. To the west, beyond Newtonmore, the Monadhliath hills gently rise up to the Munro-listed 3,070 ft. – *A' Chailleach* (the Old Woman) which does not look so high from here, being some five miles away. Close at hand, the park-like scenery of the golf course and river provide constant delight.

If the island option has been chosen, cross over the stepping-stones at the end to get back to the mainland. Please keep to the track and do not go wandering about on the golf course. Walk by the burn upstream to the footbridge, go over the railway by the bridge and carry on to the main road, and then go left, back towards the village.

There is woodland on the left, and just after the first house there is a drive down to the left. Follow the drive to where a narrow gate, on the right, leads into the woods. Through the gate there is a delightful dell with a small lochan. This is Loch Imrich, and its position here is a total surprise, and a source of pleasure to both visitors and residents alike. The loch looks like a large peat hole but is, in fact, a kettle hole; a relic of the last ice age. Surrounded by larches, and frequented by herons and sundry waterfowl, this dark pool in its wooded hollow is a little secret haven of wildlife, and is a place of quiet enchantment almost in the heart of the village. Several entry/exit points lead back onto the main street.

WALK 2

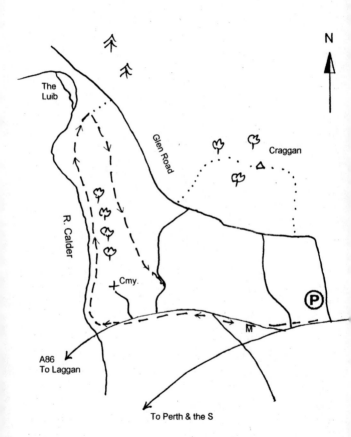

Glen Banchor and the Luib

SOME TWO HUNDRED years ago the Duke of Gordon's new Spey Bridge provided a shortcut to the Inverness-Perth road and cut out the long way round via Laggan. Also about this time, the tenants of the clachan of Milton in the Calder valley, at the foot of Glen Banchor, were being displaced to make way for sheep; they were moved to the growing settlement downstream by the Spey. So Newtonmore is, literally, the early 19th century 'new town on the moor'. The old buildings of Milton crumbled and fell down, and now only a few scattered green mounds remain on the old pastures at the entrance to Glen Banchor.

Just before the Calder Bridge on the Laggan road, at the south end of the village, a sign on the right – in both Gaelic and English – points the way to St Bride's Graveyard, which is on the site of the early Christian cell of St Bridget. This is a famous place in the Highlands as a result of a 19th century court case which re-established a right of way that had been obstructed by new building on Banchor farm land.

Just to the left of the sign, a gate and stile lead down to a riverside path, which should be followed upstream past the graveyard. There is pasture on the right, and scattered woodland and the impressive bulk of Creag Dubh on the left across the rocky bed of the river. Beyond the graveyard the path rises steeply as it climbs up the banking cut by the glacial melt water when the river was a much larger stream many thousands of years ago. At the top of the rise, another path is joined and followed to the left onto the escarpment high above the river. It is worth pausing here to look back at the delightful prospect that has unfolded with the gain in height.

The steep wooded bank on the left is opposed by the lower slopes of Creag Dubh, and the whole is divided by the straight flight of the river and garnished with a varied deciduous woodland. The background hills on Nuide Moss complete a delightful picture. The path now enters a wonderful area of birch woodland that is a sheer delight. Birdsong fills the air, and dappled sunlight falls on the path that winds gently through the trees. There is a rich understory, mainly of bilberries and ferns, and below, the river on its rocky bed crashes along in a seemingly endless succession of little waterfalls and cascades; the rocky banks have been sculpted into surreal shapes by the rapidly flowing water. There is a well-placed seat, and by the seat a break in the path leads down to the riverside – do take great care – where there is an excellent view of one of the more spectacular falls.

The path descends gently through the woodland which, like all good things, eventually comes to an end. The river bears off to the left, to the site of the old mill, and the way continues over open rough pasture and through a gate to where a track to the right climbs steeply up an eroded bank of boulder clay. At the top it joins up with the single-track road into Glen Banchor.

There is another magnificent view from here. Immediately below is the *luib* (bend) where the river curves round on its exit from Glen Banchor. The bend is bisected by the white slash of an ancient leat, which provided water to power the mill that once stood on the flat pasture, but there is nothing here now other than a few grassy mounds and some jumbled stones, backed by the wooded magnificence of Creag Dubh. To the east, the river and the glen stand revealed for the first time in all their majesty as they run straight into the heart of the mountains. There is a wealth of interesting plants in the turf, and pride of place probably goes to the uncommon alpine *Antenaria dioica* – mountain everlasting – which forms widespread pink patches in the grass in June and July.

There is a finger post by the road and a couple of options are open for the return. A path to the right follows the river along the top of the escarpment and leads back down to the Laggan road not far from the start of the riverside path. Or follow Glen Road back down into the village.

This is a very short walk of about three miles that can be enjoyed as an after-dinner stroll for an hour or so on a pleasant spring evening, but is easily extended to be enjoyed for half a day.

WALK 3

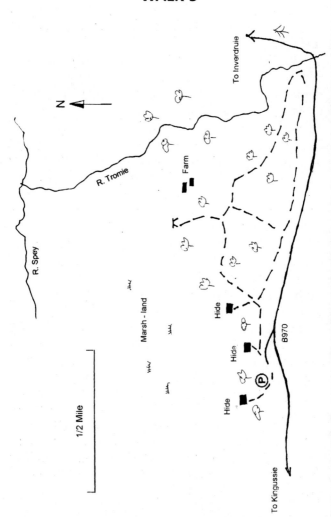

Insh Marshes RSPB Reserve

WITH AN AREA of some twenty-five square miles, the Insh Marshes reserve between Kingussie and Kincraig is probably the largest, and is certainly the most important, flood plain wetland in Britain. It is also unusual in that it comprises a unique mix of marsh and fen. Part of the River Spey SAC, it is an SSSI on its own merits, and it supports an astonishing variety of mammals, birds, insects and plants. There are many access points, and trails at Lynchlaggan, north of Insh on the B970, and at Invertromie RSPB reserve, where there is a car park off the B970, two miles from Kingussie.

If in the vicinity, whether going for a walk or not, it is worth stopping off here for a while because there is always something of interest to be seen from the information viewpoint by the car park. For a longer visit there is a choice of two hides: Gordonhall to the west and Invertromie to the east of the car park. In summer there is a guided walk with the Warden at 2.00 pm every Thursday.

A sign-posted trail offers an absorbing three-mile walk through a superb natural deciduous woodland of birch scrub with locally abundant aspen, hazel, rowan and bird cherry. There is also plenty of juniper, with the odd blackthorn or broom, and some other scrubland plants. In summer there is a wealth of orchids in the riverside grassland.

From the car park go up the steps towards the information viewpoint, and follow the fingerpost to the right in the direction of the Invertromie hide. The path goes roughly northeast through the woods, following the edge of a low escarpment that was the riverbank in the immediately post-glacial era. By keeping straight on and ignoring the branches to the right, the path leads, in about half a mile, to a picnic area at the edge of the escarpment. There are extensive views over the pastures of Invertromie Farm towards Loch Insh to the northeast, and in the other direction the flood plain can be scanned as far as Ruthven Barracks. This is a delightful spot, and once installed there will probably be no great urge to move for some considerable time. Binoculars are desirable; look out for geese and hen harriers, and the occasional osprey.

Return on the original path, and take the first branch to the left. This meanders over the farmland for about three quarters of a mile to the River Tromie, just below the settlement of Drumguish, which produces an excellent, if little known, Speyside malt whisky – it can be bought at Kincraig and the general store in Kingussie. The farmland about here is a hot spot for wildflowers and butterflies. There are dippers and otters in the river, and roe deer are often seen grazing about the reserve. Moving away from the river, the path veers round to the west and climbs gently onto a low moorland with more birch scrub. The original path is joined after about a mile and should be followed to the left, back to the information point.

In the woods here there are redstarts, flycatchers,

pipits and warblers, and in the appropriate seasons the wetland is home to a fantastic variety of wildfowl, whooper swans and waders. There are frequent sightings of a great many birds of prey, and an osprey may fly by at any time in the summer. The woodland, although deciduous, supports a number of red squirrels, which have come to appreciate the hazelnut bounty in the autumn. This walk of no more than three miles is certainly worth half a day, but if there is some of the more unusual birdlife about, a whole day here seems to pass surprisingly quickly.

WALK 4

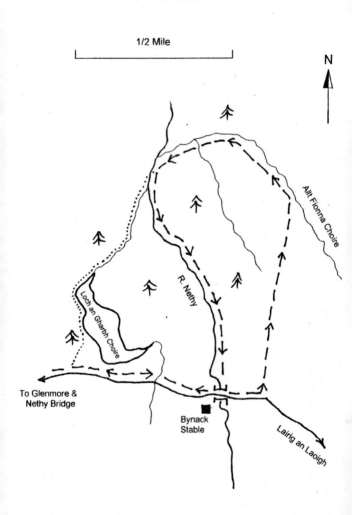

Strath Nethy

ON THE NORTHEAST slopes of Cairngorm, not far below the summit, Marquis's Well is a perpetual spring that takes its name from the Marquis of Huntly, who is said to have paused here for refreshment whilst pursuing the vanquished Earl of Argyll in 1594. The spring adds its water to the small stream flowing from the broad hollow of Ciste Mhearad, where snow often lies far into the summer. The deep and narrow valley of Strath Nethy, which runs north from the watershed by Loch Avon, receives the water from this, and from the many other streams rising in the mountains on either hand; at Bynack Stable, only four miles from its source, the Nethy is already a significant stream.

Bynack Stable heralds a dramatic change of scenery, and the mountains seem to simply melt away. The country to the north is an undulating mass of drumlins and general glacial till that makes for an interesting landscape. This was once the bed of a glacial lake, and the low hills were deposited from water flowing under melting ice. They now form a wonderful moorland of heather and other ericaceous plants, with many ancient trees, rocky outcrops, and little lochans here and there. This is the old Caledonian forest at its best, and it is a delightful place in which to walk, but the going is never very easy. The river flows north across the moor, and in many places it has carved deep and interesting gorges. About two miles beyond Bynack Stable it enters Abernethy Forest, and from there to its confluence with the Spey it flows through a dense and ancient woodland.

This walk is an interesting excursion along the trackless middle reaches of the river in the vicinity of the old 'Thieves Road'. There is some doubt as to the course of the old track way, and it is now almost entirely lost in the overgrowth of the passing years. What is certain is that the wild and unspoilt appearance of the land here is an illusion, and the countryside all about is a post-industrial landscape of the 18th and 19th centuries, when the area was extensively worked for timber extraction.

Take the road out of Glenmore to Glenmore Lodge, where there is parking for a few cars by the gate on the forest road – please do not obstruct the gate. Carry on through the glen, past the Green Lochan, heading towards Ryvoan Bothy. After about two miles there is a parting of the ways and a stony road goes off to the right. Follow this for about another mile to where there is a signpost for Braemar and a bridge over the Nethy, which is a swift and turbulent stream. Cross the bridge and follow the well-trodden path uphill for about a quarter of a mile to a point where it bends sharply to the right. At this point leave the path and strike out to the left over the rough moorland, heading a little east of north, and following a slight declivity that descends gently northwards as a vaguely defined ridge. Walk carefully because the heather hides the boulders that are abundant on these moors.

The Ordnance Survey Landranger map shows a path starting (or finishing) in the middle of nowhere at NJ026116, where it coincides with the Allt Fionna Choire that rises on the north side of An Lurg. Bear over to the right and aim to drop into the valley by the stream, where the going is a lot easier. The track, shown on the map but hardly evident on the ground, is the limb of the Lairig an Laoigh that runs south from Forest Lodge. It is evidently little used nowadays, unlike its sister track from Glenmore. Follow the *allt* downstream towards the great deer fence that runs across the forest from west to east. Before the fence is reached the stream, which here runs over a broad and stony bed, turns sharply to the west, and should be followed to its junction with the Nethy.

Away to the right, the flank of Carn Bheadhair is broken by the deep and inviting glacial overflow channels of *Eag a Chait* and *Eag a Mhadaidh* (Cat Notch and Fox Notch). But the high hills seem very far away, and there is only a rough, stony and sparsely wooded moorland here. The scenery all about is a delight, and there is a wonderful sense of freedom after a few days spent within the confines of the mountains. The trees, both dead and alive, are small and not particularly numerous, but there is a wild and untamed quality about the landscape here that is really quite invigorating.

Follow the Nethy upstream, keeping to the bank high above the stream, and enjoy some wonderful river scenery as the river crashes down through a seemingly endless succession of little canyons, gorges, cascades and waterfalls. All too soon, the bridge by the squalid bothy will be reached, and the return is by the track through Glenmore. Only about ten miles in all, but a whole day is needed to enjoy the walk in full. As an alternative finish to the walk, about a hundred yards south of the point where the Nethy is joined, near to the deer fence, a small stream merges with the river from the right (NJ021118). This is Caochan a' Bhric, which flows out of Loch a' Gharbh-choire, and it is an interesting variation to follow this upstream through a shallow canyon to the loch, and from there on to the rough road, where the way is to the right for Glenmore. See Walk 8 for more information.

PART TWO

Lochs and Lochans

HAGGIS AND HOGMANAY are synonymous with Scotland, and so are lochs and lochans. The mountain scenery of this enchanted land is world renowned, and a mountain scene is always better when it is set off by a loch. In Scotland one is almost spoilt for choice, and there is a stretch of water close at hand virtually everywhere in the Highlands.

The natural lochs of Scotland are usually features of the following kinds:

- Rift Lakes, which are formed by earth movement or faulting. The Great Glen and Loch Ness are examples of these known to everyone.

- Glacial lakes, cut and scraped by the chiselling action of the moving ice. Loch Avon and Loch Einich are classic examples.

- Kettle holes, formed when an ice-plug, embedded in sand and gravel, melted and left behind a water-filled cavity. Loch Morlich is a perfect specimen, and Loch Insh may be another.

Glacial and rift lakes tend to be long in relation to their width, and they are usually steep sided and very deep. The quoted lochs are extreme examples, but most lochs are glacial lakes and will therefore have these characteristics to some degree. It should be noted that a type of small glacial lake, usually round in shape and rarely deep, is often found in rocky corries. It is always called a lochan in Scotland. More usually, lochans lie in areas of glacial debris and are, in effect, large ponds.

Kettle holes are much less common, and they tend to be either squarish, or virtually circular. They are usually quite shallow, and often lie somewhat apart from the mountains. Loch Leven is probably the best generally known example. There is another kind of still water pool called a Peat Hole, which looks like a lochan, but is not glacial, and is not a kettle hole. Why and how they are formed is a bit of a mystery, but they tend to crop up in areas of sphagnum peat blanket when the peat is locally washed away. There are several examples near Ryvoan Bothy. The adjacent Loch a' Gharbh-choire looks like a very large peat hole, but it is probably artificial. It could have been created when the stream was dammed to form a reservoir for logging operations in the 18th and 19th centuries, and it was certainly much larger then. A little dam remains, and the loch would probably dry up completely if it were removed.

There is really not much sense in trying to explain what constitutes a loch, nor how lochs differ from lochans; the differences are debatable and somewhat academic. We all know one when we see one, and we all have our own ideas, so what would be the point? The important thing is to recognise that lochs and lochans are fascinating and captivating features in their own right. They are all different, and they all have something to offer the interested visitor. They attract fishermen, both human and avian. They have a distinct and distinctly varied fauna and flora, which appeal to all sorts of naturalists, and they are as varied in their appearances as they are in their locations. They are photogenic to a high degree.

There is a great deal of real pleasure and a rare contentment to be had from simply sitting on the banks of any sort of loch on a balmy late-spring day. The sky seems very high, the clouds float gently, and there is a particular kind of freshness in the air. There is usually the sound of water running somewhere close by, and an occasional plop as a hungry trout leaps out of the water in pursuit of a passing gnat. Sunlight flashes on the iridescent bodies of the damselflies, and the buzz and drone of busy bees and midges mingle with the gentle chobbeling of sundry waterfowl that are rooting in the reeds at the water margins. All these sights and sounds emphasise the sense of isolation from the rest of a rather frantic mankind. It is sheer bliss.

The following six walks visit some of the many lochs and lochans in the area. None of the lochs is very big, but all are extremely pleasant places. All of the walks are decidedly gentle, but the visit to the Lochans of Inshriach needs good weather and a fair bit of stamina if the ascent of Creag Far-leitire is to be included.

WALK 5

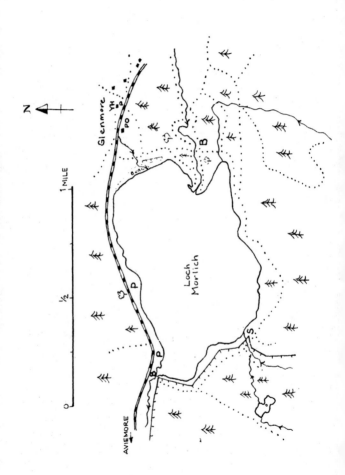

Loch Morlich

A CIRCUIT OF the loch may seem to be just about the least interesting local walk in Glenmore. One side is bounded by the ski road, and forestry tracks flank two other sides. Only at the Allt Mor beachhead are there un-metalled paths expressly for walking on. As with many other things in this life, appearances can be deceptive: the walk is not devoid of interest and it is worth doing at least once. It is another piece in the geological jigsaw that has produced such a varied and attractive landscape. Take it slowly, and enjoy the wildlife and the views.

Loch Morlich is a classic example of a kettle-hole – the final resting place of a very large lump of ice – the dying remnant of the last glacier in Glenmore. It is amazing that geologists know this even though it happened such a long time ago. It explains the peculiar contours of the bottom of the loch, which is generally shallow, except at the east end where a submarine cliff, with a slope of 1 in 4, falls 50 feet into the hole. The geological processes continue, and the edge of the cliff is advancing slowly westwards as the Allt Mor continually washes in a fresh supply of sand and gravel. Several acres of new beach have been added this century, and the rate of change is so rapid that differences can be noticed from year to year. One day, perhaps, the loch will be no more; it will be filled up with detritus from the hills; and Cairngorm could be by then a mere shadow of its present self, and people would walk on it instead of up it.

The loch has an appeal of its own, and it occupies a picturesque and sheltered setting at the west end of Glen More. Surrounded by pinewoods, it nestles at the foot of the great northern corries of the Cairngorm massif, and it is an excellent place to observe Homo Sapiens as people busily enjoy their holiday in, on, or about the water. The red-gold sands provide a substitute seaside for countless children – young, middle-aged and elderly. The loch itself supports all sorts of quiet water sports – no noisy power boats and no water skiing – and the beach by the Allt Mor estuary is often thronged with optimistic anglers who stand like a row of mechanical toys as they hope – usually in vain – to hook an educated trout or pike. An occasional band of bewildered schoolchildren, with glazed eyes and doodled clipboards, follows the stream and an anxious teacher in search of O, A, or Higher level excellence – at least *they* will know all about kettle holes. The country is big enough to absorb them all, and the surrounding woods and marshlands provide plenty of scope for the nature-loving walker or idler.

The best times for a walk here are early or late in the day, and early morning has the edge so far as birdlife is concerned. Deer, both red and roe, seem to be seen more often in the late evening, although they are often all over the place just after dawn in late spring. It is appropriate to mention here that deer watching is an activity not normally associated with this kind of walking. It usually involves a lot of patient waiting, in the middle of the night, in a particular spot which deer are known to frequent. Park by the Forest Enterprise Centre in Glenmore, cross the road, and go through the caravan/camp site to the lakeshore. There is a large, clean, attractive, very sandy, and extremely popular beach at this end of the loch. Follow the shoreline to the left, to the Allt Mor estuary. The area of beach here is growing all the time. The actual entry point into the loch can be seen to vary from year to year, which is geology in action. To the layman it is about as exciting as watching paint dry.

Go to the footbridge, upstream to the left, cross to the other bank, and follow the stream down to the shore again. There is a marked change of atmosphere here, and this part of the loch is a quiet, shallow and reedy bay that looks very 'pikey' to any fisherman. The land here is often under water in the cold half of the year, and even in summer it can be a bit swampy.

Follow the shoreline, at first by the water's edge, and then through the woodland to a point where a path goes steeply uphill to the left. This leads onto a forest road that goes round the back of the loch, and the open aspect to the west, over the loch, is a good place from which to see some wonderful sunsets. This is also a good place to see widgeon, which seem to favour this quiet bay.

The view to the left is rather depressing following the virtually clear felling of large tracts of alien conifers. But cheer up: this is the beginning of a scheme to regenerate the Caledonian forest hereabouts, and it will be a pleasant woodland again in about fifty years.

Look closely, however, and the seedling trees of the new generation will be seen to be Sitka spruce, or some of the other species of alien conifers. This is not what is supposed to happen, but man's attempts to control nature have rarely been successful!

Go right along the forest road, which here runs high above the loch, and where the tree clearance has opened up splendid views across to the Kincardine hills. As the cleared area comes to an end the track starts to descend quite steeply through a close-planted mature woodland. Just before the deer fence, which marks the boundary with Rothiemurchus Estate (NH959089), another forest road cuts back to the left. Follow this road uphill through a woodland of closely planted Scots pine, with the occasional downy birch for contrast. The track is of compacted pink granite gravel, which is crunchy underfoot and makes for pleasant walking. It contours around the foot of a sizeable knoll for about a quarter of a mile to where a sign points to Serpents Loch, on the left. The picnic table by the loch is set in a little glade, and it is not only used by humans. The ground here is literally completely covered with the debris of pinecones left by banqueting red squirrels. It is an idyllic spot, not to be missed.

Retrace the path back to the Rothiemurchus fence, and cross the stile – there is a special gate for dogs. It will be obvious that the fence is not just a boundary between two estates, it also separates two entirely different forms of woodland. The pleasant but rather formal planting of the Forestry Commission is here replaced with a more open and quite delightful natural tract of old forest. The road may be rougher, but there is more sky – and more sun – and the Scots pines are joined by juniper scrub and a lot more silver and downy birch.

The loch can be seen again, over to the right, and do keep an eye on the sky – this is a favourite locale for fishing osprey. At the junction with the gravel road to Rothiemurchus Lodge, the route is followed to the right, to the Bailey Bridge crossing the Luineag at its out-flow from the loch. The way back to Glenmore follows the motor road, but that is not as bad as it may seem. There is always a pleasant grass verge, and there are many diversions by the loch and away from the road.

This is a basic walk of about four miles, but there is a veritable maze of paths and tracks behind the beach at the east end of the loch, and it is fun to use the Ordnance map and make up your own private routes. They can cover a seemingly endless variety of new forest clearance, old woodland, loch side, streamside, meadow-land, scrubland and marshland.

There are opportunities here for observing almost every type of life, and subjects range from humans, arguably at the top of the animal kingdom, down to tiny wood mites, which are almost certainly at the bot-tom. Interesting woodland birds abound, and water-fowl and plant life are abundant. Or just sit on a log and think; but do be wary of the wood ants – they bite like mad. Above all, do not sit on an anthill – yes, it has happened, and they can seem inviting if you haven't seen them before.

WALK 6

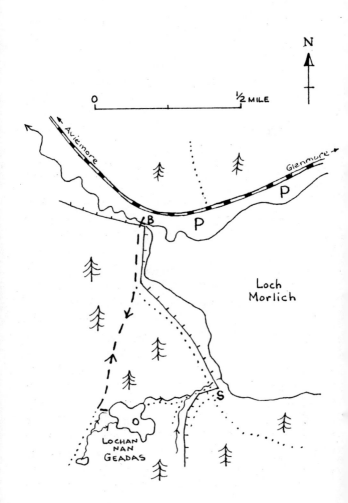

Lochan nan Geadas

JUST UP THE road to Rothiemurchus Lodge, easily missed by the unknowing, and overshadowed by Loch Morlich, its nearby big and famous neighbour, this little lochan has a charm and beauty of its own. It is a minor Mecca for knowledgeable bird-watchers, and one of its greatest charms is that it is impossible to forecast what will be there.

Cross the bridge at the west end of Loch Morlich (NH959096) and follow the track towards Rothiemurchus Lodge. At the point where the tracks divide keep to the right on the main track, and after about a mile, just before a flooded gravel pit, look for a break in the young trees to the left. The lochan is fed by a little stream, and is well hidden. There is a very pleasant resting-place beneath the branches of a venerable old Scots pine, round to the left from the approach path, and it makes a most convenient natural hide from which to watch the comings and goings of the birds.

On the opposite shore there are a couple of low hides that have probably been provided for the concealment of wildfowlers, but serve equally well for bird watchers. The avian population varies with the day, not just with the season, and the following are typical: goosander in the early spring (nest boxes like upended coffins on the trees on the island), widgeon, oyster catcher and goldeneye. There is, of course, no guarantee that any particular birds, or even any birds, will be seen during any given visit, but the chances are that one will be pleasantly surprised, and the lochan is worth visiting just for its own sake. There is no such thing as a wasted day when out and about here.

This location is included with some misgivings because it is one of the author's favourite places, and it would be a shame to see a good thing ruined by the pressures of too many people. So if you should arrive and find that another has beaten you to it, then go away until some other time. Better by far to leave it for another day, rather than force the wildfowl to leave it forever.

WALK 7

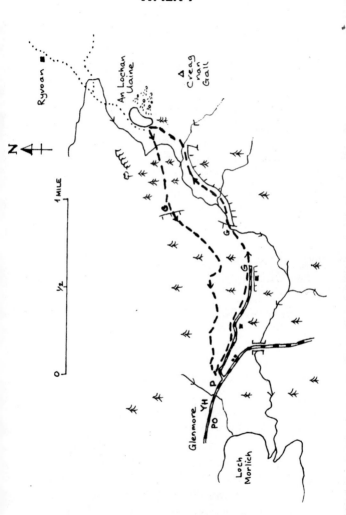

Glen More, the Green Lochan and the Primrose Path

GLENMORE IS A TINY and unpretentious hamlet at the northeast corner of Loch Morlich. It comprises a post office cum café cum off-licence cum general store, a youth hostel, the Reindeer House, the Forest Enterprise centre and a chapel – at which all are welcome for a good sing on a summer Sunday evening. There is also a group of foresters' houses nearby. In the appropriate seasons the resident population is augmented by the transients at the youth hostel, on the caravan/camp site, and in the few B&B houses. These are often people who come one week for a week and want to stay on without really knowing why. They all go home, of course, but only after developing a tendency to keep coming back year after year.

Glenmore is a perfect compromise because it is relatively close to the fleshpots of Aviemore, but is remote enough to be blissfully quiet between teatime and breakfast time. It is very close to the mountains, and is an ideal place for almost any sort of outdoor holiday. One wonders why the Aviemore Centre was not built here instead – perhaps the planners got it right for once?

The ambience is overwhelmingly one of peace and tranquillity, which rubs off on the visitors. People who, at home, would hurry by without a glance, are inclined to pause and discuss the weather (inevitably), the fishing (always so-so), the walking (never too strenuous), or almost anything remote from the monotony of their normal – but seemingly all too abnormal – everyday world. If it sounds like some sort of primitive Heaven or haven in the Highlands, be assured that it is; and be thankful for simply being here.

It would be simpler if it were called Kinlochmorlich, but it isn't, and Glenmore, the hamlet, should not be confused with Glen More. To avoid confusion with its more illustrious namesake, the Great Glen, it may be well to explain that this Glen More is the open-ended valley that extends, roughly, some three or four miles from Ryvoan to the hamlet of Glenmore. It is traversed from end to end by the Thieves Road – the ancient *Rathad nam Mearlaich* – and it has the Kincardine hills on one hand and the Cairngorms on the other. It is a very small area of very great beauty, and it is worthy of far more than the cursory interest usually displayed by transients en route to places of larger size and greater renown.

This gentle walk of some four miles need take no more than a short afternoon, and it may even be accomplished as an after dinner stroll on one of those long and balmy late spring or summer evenings. Some folk can make it last all day, and the enjoyment increases in proportion. It provides a lot of very good value for very little effort.

Start from the car park by the Forest Enterprise Centre, which is just beyond the youth hostel, and on the same side of the road (NH970098). On the green here there is a large erratic boulder set in an area of

paving, and with a few planted alpines which have
survived the early morning browsing of the deer. This
is the Norwegian Stone, and it is a hallowed memorial
to the very many Norwegians of Kompani Linge who
lived and trained in this district, and who subsequently
died on operations during the last war. The present
youth hostel was the Operations Centre for the famous
Telemark raid, and the Norwegian Hostel, on the road
to New Glenmore Lodge, is built on the site of the old
Commando barracks. There is a timeless air about the
memorial, and it is refreshing to see that some people
still care – there are always fresh flowers at the base
of the stone.

Cross the green, go past the end of Reindeer House,
and follow the stretch of asphalt road to the outdoor
pursuits school at Glenmore Lodge. This modern building has taken the name which rightly belongs to Loch
Morlich Youth Hostel, the old hunting lodge of the
Dukes of Richmond and Gordon. Wainwright pointed
out that feet are always the last things to tire when tra-
versing fell and moorland. Conversely, they are always
the first things to tire when walking on tarmac, and
the truth of this assertion will be apparent during this
first half-mile or so if you walk down the road. Take
heart, for most of the way the road has a foresters'
scrape on the left hand side, and there is plenty of
interest in a walk along here. There are milk-, butter-,
louse-, and other worts, and there are newts in the
puddled tyre ruts. Where do they come from and
where do they go? (The newts, that is.)

Just beyond the Lodge, by the locked gate, about

a dozen cars can be parked in a little lay-by. Beyond the gate there is a rough forest road, and a complete change in the character of the country. The rough ground, now cleared of the serried ranks of close-planted alien conifers, is replaced by a much more open and interesting landscape. Low mounds, with birch scrub and marshy stretches in between, are plentifully dotted here and there with small Scots pines. The mounds are moraines, left behind when a large glacial lake emptied through Ryvoan. The marshy patches are all that remain of the residual lochans that originally spattered the area, but have since either drained away or silted up.

The trees here are really quite a rarity: they are some of the few remnants of the old Caledonian forest. They grow high up on the flanks of the hills that bound the pass immediately ahead, and the tree line is well above the 1,500 foot contour which is normally the limit for successful tree growth in Britain. This indicates a very sheltered site, but because of a very short growing season and poor soil fertility, the trees, whilst very old, are very small. This is a happy accident, for very large trees would be a bit overpowering in this intimate little glen.

About a mile further along the track, at the margin of the Queen's Forest, the impressive face of Creag nan Gall rises on the right. It marks the end of a low outlier from the main Cairngorm ridge but, geologically, this spur is not part of the Cairngorms at all. They are granite hills, and the rock exposed here is a form of granulite, and masses of the cold grey stone can be seen in the screes cascaded down the hillside on the right. The Creag is probably a separated chunk of the Kincardine Hills, and they, in turn, are possibly a detached arm of the Monadhliaths. It is all something of a rocky hotchpotch. As might by now be guessed, the divide, which we call the Pass of Ryvoan, is a glacial feature, and it is an extreme example of an overflow channel.

An Lochan Uaine has a dramatic setting backed by the rugged screes and trees of the Creag. Many regard this as the most beautiful of the many 'Green Lochans' of the Cairngorms. It is certainly a delightful spot in which to laze away the odd half-hour on a bonny morning. Tree lined and deeply set, the lochan is a sheltered sun trap. It gets its name because the complete lack of marine vegetation, coupled with minute flakes of mica in the clear water, makes it reflect the colour of its rocky bed, and the water is a lovely emerald green. Sometimes, in early summer, the water close inshore looks like custard. This is caused by an accumulation of pollen from the surrounding trees.

Leaving the lochan, take the faint track that strikes back across the valley towards the tree-clad hillside of Creag Loisgte. The uphill path is narrow and, in places, very steep. It also has a wealth of snags like concealed rocks and old tree roots to trip up the unwary, so do not try to sightsee on the move. Be sensible, and stop often to enjoy the views down the glen and across the great northern corries to Chalamain and beyond. This short climb can be a delight for the naturalist, and many interesting birds and plants may be seen on the warm and very sheltered hill. In late spring there is an abundance of primroses.

The path eventually emerges onto a pink gritted forest road which is followed down to the car park, and the many cleared rides to the left offer pleasant views down to the Ryvoan track and beyond. It may be noted that some of the remaining mature trees are really quite beautiful. The trees here are also home to many crested tits, and a chance to see these tiny rarities should add to the attractions of this delightful walk.

WALK 8

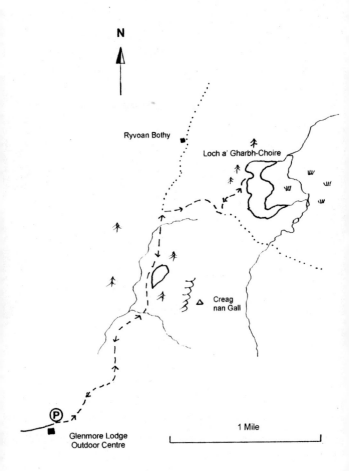

N

Ryvoan Bothy

Loch a' Gharbh-Choire

Creag
nan Gall

Glenmore Lodge
Outdoor Centre

1 Mile

Loch a' Gharbh-choire

ONE OF THE most delightful of the multitude of lochs in the area is largely artificial, being a product of the logging industry, which was one of the major local employers in the three hundred years up to 1900. In the mid-19th century this was known as the Garrochir Dam, and it was just one of a large network of floating dams in the area. Tree trunks cut down in the adjacent woodlands were tipped into the streambeds, and when sufficient water had built up in the dams the sluices were opened. The resulting flood then carried the logs down to the Rivers Nethy and Spey, from where they could be moved into the saw and boring mills, or assembled into rafts to be floated downstream to the shipyards at Kingston. The dams lapsed into disuse when the roads were improved and when the railways came in the late 1850s.

There was probably a little lochan here originally, fed by the stream which emerges from the corrie of the same name at the end of the Cairngorm north ridge. But a walk around the moorland here will reveal the remains of a large dam, and the existing dammed outlet from the loch, at the eastern extremity of the northern arm, is probably the only thing that prevents this exquisite little stretch of water reverting to a bog.

An Lochan Uaine has a dramatic setting, and it is certainly a delightful spot in which to laze away the odd half-hour with a cup of coffee on a bonny morning.

Tree lined and deeply set, the lochan is a sheltered suntrap with attractive beaches of coarse granite sand. To the west of the path, opposite the lochan, the low lying and boggy ground is all that remains of yet another floating dam that was used to take timber into Glenmore.

Beyond the lochan, with Ryvoan bothy on the skyline, and where the tracks divide, take the right branch and carry on to the top of the rise where, on the left, a track starts off to the left through the heather. There may even be a little pile of stones. There is no definite track to the Loch, just keep to the high ground whilst tracking to the east and the loch will be reached quite soon. It is often not realised that serious idling is a serious business, and it has to be learnt and developed over a long time, and this little lochan is the perfect place to start. The place to aim for is a little tree studded peninsula about NJ012112, where the thin soil on a rocky bed provides a perfect spot for lounging and contemplating the pleasures of this particular place. The loch deserves more than just a casual visit, and it will repay some little investigation. A clockwise circuit will reveal the sluice that controls the present level, and on the eastern side, bounded by streams, there is a rather swampy area with the remains of the log-floaters' old dams. The southern arm of the loch has many rotting tree stumps that are home to the gulls that choose to nest here in the early summer. All in all it is a picturesque and interesting place that adequately repays a little attention.

The adjoining countryside is also worth a bit of

exploration, and has many delightful secret dells and natural rock gardens. A walk along the streamside from NJ021118 to the loch could provide an interesting alternative finish to the Strath Nethy route – Walk 4.

WALK 9

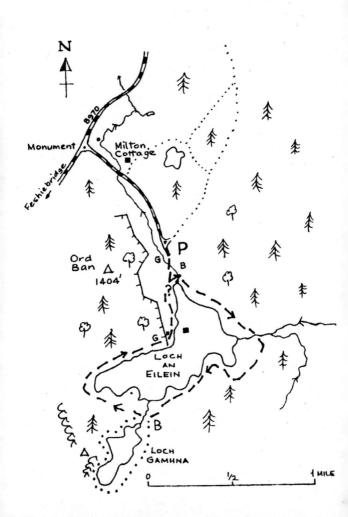

Loch an Eilein

LOCH AN EILEIN has nearly everything: in an idyllic setting in an ancient woodland, it is backed by dramatic crags. It has a varied and most attractive shoreline and a romantic ruined castle on an island. It is possible to drive there from both north and south on good if somewhat narrow roads, and it is also possible to walk there almost entirely on footpaths. There is a large car park, a visitor centre, a toilet block, and a nature trail on adequate but not overdone paths. One could go on and on but, in a nutshell, Loch an Eilein has virtually all that the casual tripper could desire. Despite this, and notwithstanding its consequent popularity, it remains an extraordinarily pleasant place.

The loch lies in the largest surviving fragment of the old Caledonian forest, and here, in Rothiemurchus, there is a most varied and interesting range of wildlife to be seen by the experienced and careful observer. The casual visitor is unlikely to see much of the larger animals, but roe deer and red squirrels are not uncommon, and there are always plenty of butterflies, birds, and interesting plants. In winter the local sledge racers use the area to train their husky teams. A short walk around the loch is, perhaps, the perfect introduction to Rothiemurchus forest. It is always an enjoyable experience, and it is a good alternative to the hills if the clouds are down, or if it is too hot to be away from shade.

Across the way from the Ranger Centre at Inverdruie (NH901110) a minor road goes roughly southeast. After about a mile, by the Martineau memorial, there is a branch road to the left that goes down to the car park by the loch (NH898086). The route is sign-posted.

Some time spent in the Visitor Centre, *before* going anywhere else, will greatly increase the pleasure of a walk here. Then take the track to the left for a clock-wise circuit of the loch. At the north end of the loch the land is relatively open, and this shore can offer good views of the ruin, which is close enough for pho-tographs, but not so close that it dominates the view.

This little castle is reputed to have been a 14th or 15th century stronghold of one Alexander Stewart, the legendary Wolf of Badenoch, a local warlord and notorious bandit. A bastard son of the Scottish king Bruce II, he was infamous for having sacked and burned the cathedral of Elgin. The castle is also known to have been the last refuge of the osprey until it was finally harried out of existence as a British nesting species about the end of the 19th century. The birds have had the last laugh. Their numbers have grown since their re-introduction at Loch Garten in the 1950s, and ospreys now fish the loch again. Arriving in April and leaving in September, some birds nest in the locality, and they spend the summer in Rothiemurchus. Crested tits and crossbills are less spectacular birds that also nest here, but they are also rarities, and will be of equal interest to keen birdwatchers.

Birds are only one aspect of the very varied wild-life to be seen in the vicinity, and there are botanical surprises too. For example, the yellow figwort is a plant that has really no business to be here at all; supposedly it is found mainly in southern England, but a very healthy specimen was in flower in a crevice in a wall by the visitor centre not all that long ago. There are many fungi in the birch thickets on the west side of the loch, and one of the bracket fungi – *Fomes fomentarius* – occurs in only one other locality in Britain, in the Kentish woodlands. It was avidly collected many years ago because the dried and shredded flesh was ideal kindling in a tinderbox, and there was also a short-lived Victorian vogue for drawings executed on the parchment-like surface of the gills.

The ruined buildings around the visitor centre are all that remain of a timber industry that flourished here in the 18th century, and many of the older trees date from around this time. They may be found at the southern end of the loch, and some of them would have been mere seedlings at the time of the '45. It may be of interest to note that a cross-sectioned trunk of one of these trees with various significant dates marked on the growth rings can be seen in the Forest Enterprise Centre in Glenmore.

It is possible to make a diversion at the south end of the loch and stroll around little Loch Gamhna. This is also a glacial loch, but must be at a late stage in its development because it is now very shallow and it has a totally different character to its relative next door. Separated by only a few yards in distance, they are worlds apart in atmosphere and appearance. In summer the water lilies here are a picture.

The whole of the Loch an Eilein reserve is included in the National Nature Reserve by agreement with the Rothiemurchus Estate, and visitors have access to the network of private paths and rights of way that criss-cross the forest of Rothiemurchus. It is an enchanting place, and is totally unlike the common concept of a conifer forest. This sylvan wilderness is a place of great beauty, and it is a sanctuary for many species that are rare or extinct elsewhere. It is a primeval paradise that can occupy and entertain the artist, naturalist, photographer, or mere wanderer, for a very long time.

WALK 10

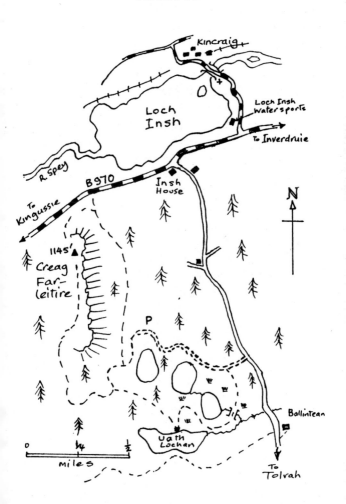

The Secret Lochans of Inshriach

NOT ALL WALKERS here are visitors, and it is sometimes forgotten that the local populace, too, greatly appreciates and enjoys the wealth of wonderful country on their doorstep. They also have the advantage of an intimate knowledge of the locality – something that the seasonal visitor doesn't have. So it may be expected that most places have a number of goodies known only to locals, and rarely visited by people from outwith the area. This walk is one of them. It is based on a Forest Enterprise recreation area called Uath Lochans, but to the inhabitants of Newtonmore, Kingussie and Kincraig it is known simply as 'The Four Lochs'.

About one mile down the minor road to Ballintean and Tolvah, that runs south from its junction with B970 by the old, Telford-built, manse of Insh House, there is an insignificant rough track to the right. A Forest Enterprise signboard (NH839022) advertises the site, and the track leads to a delightful glade where extensive parking and a pleasant picnic area have been provided. The walk starts and ends here, and it passes through a planting of Lodgepole pine set within extensive stands of the old Caledonian pinewoods of Inshriach. It should help to dispel the notion that all modern forestry is both ugly and sterile. The local forests in Badenoch and Strathspey are often something of a hybrid, consisting of a hard core of ancient woodland within an area of new conifer plantings. In this context 'new' is relative, and much of the timber was planted in the immediate post-war years. It has now matured, and widespread felling is in progress here and there, particularly in the Queen's Forest and in the adjoining woodland in Glenmore, where any one of the stacks of newly cut timber will provide an opportunity for a ring count. It takes only a few moments to see that most of the trees are about thirty to fifty years old, but the odd Scots pine log of equal size amongst the lumber will be very much older. This is a simple, yet vivid, illustration of the economic argument for the widespread planting of spruce, larch and fir.

Rock Wood has, so far, been spared the woodman's axe, and Uath Lochan – literally the dreadful, or frightful pool – totally belies its name. It is one of the hidden delights of the area, and a complete circuit of the trail is a short walk of some two miles. It is an ideal early evening stroll, and early evening in summer can have a particular kind of magic here. But 'short', as in 'walks', is entirely personal and, at almost any time, it is possible to spend an enjoyable day here just pottering about the moor and woodland, watching wildlife, and sampling the delights of the waterside and the adjacent heights of Creag Far-leitire. The lochans are connected by a path, which meanders through the ancient woodland of Scots pine to a hide that has been beautifully sited on the north shore of Uath Lochan. This is an extensive, secluded and sheltered stretch of water that has the inevitable resident population of mallard. It is also a magnet for migratory wildfowl and waders of many kinds. And do keep a lookout for fishing ospreys: a pair of these magnificent birds now nests by Loch Insh, and an osprey could literally drop in at any time. Keen bird-watchers will probably spend a long time here.

The path turns back to the north, veers right through a patch of birch wood, and then traverses a wide-open and reedy scrubland. Bog myrtle is everywhere, and its heady scent fills the air in the hot sunshine. As might be expected, there is a wealth of sphagnum, and there is also a magnificent stretch of phragmites reed swamp. These tall and graceful reeds move ceaselessly in the slightest breeze, and the feathery bronze heads and ochre stems provide a restrained but colourful contrast to the chocolate brown waters of the many little peat holes on the moor.

Don't worry; there will be no wet feet because the path traverses a well-constructed and slightly elevated duck-board walkway over the really boggy bits. The way continues past a small lochan, and then joins the entrance track, which should be followed to the left, to the car park. On the way it passes by the other two lochans, which nestle in an open plantation of Lodgepole pine.

To the west of the woodland, Creag Far-leitire provides a back-drop to the trail. It is incredibly dramatic, and is the epitome of all those fearsomely steep and precipitous wooded crags in 18th and 19th century prints. A track branches off to the right from the main path and after a few hundred yards, a green-topped post marks a minor track that goes off through the woods to the right. It goes east to the edge of the crags where a few clearings look out over the lochans to the Glen Feshie hills. The exposure, like the views, is sensational in places, so do be extremely careful. The track continues to the north to a clearing with a seat that looks out over Kincraig. It then winds round, onwards and upwards to the summit at 1,145 ft. This should be a bosky belvedere, but it is not: there are just too many trees, and the Creag is not a particularly good viewpoint. However, it is not all doom and gloom, and there is a reasonable prospect of Newtonmore's Creag Dubh, and a gap that looks out over Loch Insh and Kincraig towards Aviemore to the northwest. From the summit, down the easier gradient to the north, a sinuous path snakes to the car park.

Towards the end of the day when the light is soft, when there is just a little wreath of mist, and when the blackish background conifers, silhouetted against the sky, are subtly back-lit by a low and rosy glowing sun, this is a most enchanting place. Glory in the blissful silence of it all, and enjoy the peace and quiet, alone in the forest with only deer and other wildlife for company. This is the stuff of pleasant dreams, and of imperishable memories.

PART THREE

Glen Feshie

THIS LITTLE-VISITED gem, which runs down the western margins of the Cairngorms, is one of Scotland's loveliest glens. There is a slow transition from the bleak and hostile tundra of Britain's highest mountain plateau to the soft and verdant pastures by the riverside. Typical of the Grampians, the landscape bears the unmistakable stamp of its glacial past. There is a marked contrast, however, between this most delightful of river valleys – which provides a lonely but lovely walking route from Kingussie to Braemar – and those other north-south routes, the Lairig an Laoigh and the Lairig Ghru.

A broad strath of the softest green is dotted, here and there, with the brown and ochre mounds of ancient drumlins. Nicely rounded hills, with rocky scars and outcrops, provide a dramatic backdrop for the trees. Gnarled and knotted old Scots pines alternate with weeping birch and prickly gorse and junipers, and the river is always close at hand. In places there may be up to a dozen separate streams, and little lawns of lush green grass provide ideal picnic spots between the rills of icy water draining down from *An Moine Mhor* – The Great Moss.

English visitors who know The Lakes will feel very much at home because there is a very 'Lakeland' feel about it all, but the resemblance ends with that. There is a marked lack of tourist hordes, and a very different scale: Glen Feshie is simply vast. It provides plenty of space and plenty of scope for artists, walkers, naturalists, botanists, birdwatchers, and sundry other discerning folk. Seekers after solitude, they all can find here something very special in the peace and quiet, and in the absence of the frenzied activity that is now so apparent in other parts of the Cairngorms

About 10 miles above Feshiebridge there is a confluence of several streams, and the Feshie turns sharply up towards the east. The valley walls pull sharply in, and the valley floor begins to climb towards the watershed. This is reached at about 1,800 feet, where Feshie merges into Mar and meets the headwaters of the Geldie Burn.

Other than the long way round via Tomintoul, this is the only easy passage between Speyside and Deeside. From time to time there have been proposals for a road through the glen, and the route was first surveyed by General Wade in the 18th century. More recent was a survey in the 1950s, but high cost and low usage now mean that the glen will be left alone, and it could long remain a haven for those seeking a particular kind of peace.

The wilderness is more apparent than real, and there was much activity here in the past. The glen has been lived in since early times, and one authority derives the name from Feshor Fora, a 10th century Pictish chief. There are the remains of several farms, and there once was a thriving timber industry. Most of the old pines of Caledon were felled during World War 1, but some well thought-out schemes of reforestation are putting matters right. There are still many areas of pleasant mature woodland, with a mixture of both coniferous and broad-leaved trees, and the glen is famous for its deer – it is not uncommon to see herds of several hundred moving on the hill.

It is important to remember that deer stalking goes on here in the appropriate season. Between 15 August and 31 January walkers should not go on the hills here without first talking to the Stalker. He can be found at Carnachuin, by the Monument (NN845939), a little to the North of Feshie Lodge.

Access can be something of a problem. It is not a matter of getting onto the land – that is easy – it is the sheer difficulty of getting there at all. The good walking starts about 5 miles south of Feshiebridge, and that is at least 10 miles from both Aviemore and Kingussie. The best option is to drive down the road on the east side of the river to Achlean, where a car can be parked in a little lay-by above, and just before, the farm (NN852976). Larger groups can hire a minibus, with driver, to deliver and collect at given times. This can be a very economical form of travel, and 10 people can do the combined round trips from Aviemore for a few pounds per head. Try Geordies Taxis – 01479 810118. Whatever the effort, whatever the time and trouble involved in getting there, one thing is certain: it will be well worthwhile. Glen Feshie is a rarity that beckons one to return time and time again.

WALK 11

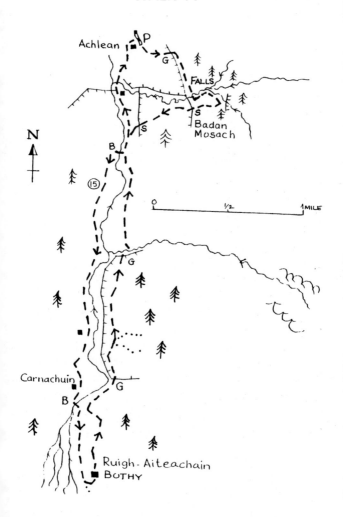

Achlean

P

G

FALLS

Badan Mosach

S

S

N

B

⑮

O   ½   1 MILE

G

Carnachuin

B

G

Ruigh - Aiteachain
BOTHY

Finnegan's Force

TO BE HONEST, there isn't a waterfall with this name – well, not in Glen Feshie – and its fabrication by a Southron is likely to raise the blood pressure of the average Gael to a level well above the local mountain tops. But the subject of this walk is so magnificent that it ought to have a name of its own, and the fact that its location is on Allt Fhearnagan should be explanation enough.

This is one of the problems with the Grampians: the magnificent is so commonplace that it is often judged unworthy of any special comment, or anything other than a cursory mention on a map. There can be no other reaon why this splendid waterfall has remained anonymous for so long. Where else would a tremendous double fall, cascading for hundreds of feet down a green and pleasant mountainside, be virtually completely ignored? This is very odd, because it is one of the most easily accessible of spectacles in this most spectacular glen. The fall is usually referred to as Badan Mosach, which is actually the name of the wooded area through which it runs, and its lack of recognition ended only recently when Louis Scott listed it in his book. It is his favourite of all the waterfalls in Scotland, and it requires very little effort to find out why.

The most convenient starting point is Achlean, where a car may be parked in the little lay-by near to the farm (NN852976). There is no doubt about the path:

it is obvious, and goes off uphill to the left before the farm. This is the start of the old 'Foxhunters' track, which leads eventually to the summit of Carn Ban Mor. It provides a long but relatively painless route to the Sgorans, and has been a popular excursion since Victorian times; but that is a journey for another day. There is a ladder stile over the deer fence, and a branch track is then followed to the right, along the edge of the woodland, and straight to the bottom of the cascade.

This is the epitome of a romantic waterfall in a setting of sylvan delight. A leisurely climb to the top is a must, and will be carried out so slowly, and amidst surroundings of such sublime, enchanting and absorbing beauty, that the exertion will pass un-noticed as the falls are followed for several hundred feet uphill. The setting is a delight, and cries out for photographs as the sunlight filters through the cool and mature woodland of old Scots pine, and the sight and sounds of water fill the air.

Cross the primitive bridge, by the fence, and the track can then be followed up until it emerges from the forest onto the open hillside. Another track bears right, along the edge of the woodland, to the old site of an observation tower. The return track goes downhill, back to the foot of the falls, and then through a fairly new planting of Scots pine to Achleum and the river. The riverside track is then followed to the Allt, which will have to be forded, because the old footbridge has been removed. Across the stream, the track continues back to Achlean. And the 'Force'? This is a common name for a waterfall in other parts of Britain and is a relic of our Viking forbears. It is a corruption of the Scandinavian *fjors* – a waterfall – and it somehow seems appropriate in this place.

Some maps show a track from the corner of the forest, by the falls, over the moor to Achlean. Do not be tempted to take this track – it will spoil your day. The farmer at Achlean has a special brand of invective for people who come this way, and he does have a point: fences should be crossed only via stiles or gates.

This is a very short walk, and it would have satisfied Burns, who said that Scottish waterfalls were 'worth gaun a mile tae see'. The energetic may do a few more miles and cap a most enjoyable day by carrying on to Landseer's Bothy.

WALK 12

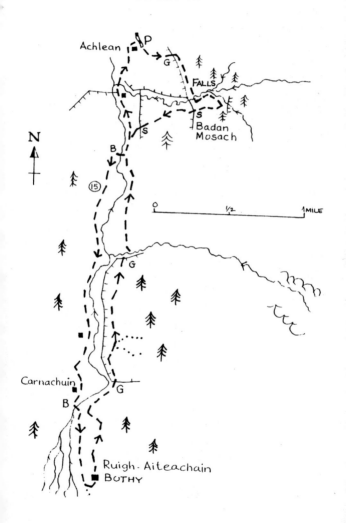

Achlean

P

G

FALLS

Badan
Mosach

S

S

N

B

⑮

B

G

G

Carnachuin

B

Ruigh · Aiteachain
BOTHY

0   ½   1 MILE

Landseer's Bothy

IN 1842 THE young Queen Victoria and her Consort made their first visit to Scotland. Other visits followed, and they quite naturally came to love the place. Indeed, the spell was so strong that they had to have a permanent house there, and in 1848, having rejected Ardverikie as too wet and too midge ridden, they acquired the Duke of Fife's old hunting lodge at Balmoral. Thus started the tradition of regal summer holidays in the Highlands.

The Queen was very artistic, and had drawing and painting lessons from a number of artists – Edward Lear was an early tutor, and William Leitch is the one who figured most in this role during her Balmoral days. She also had a great appreciation of the beauty of her countryside, and wished to have a permanent record of the time she spent here with her beloved Albert. Over the years they compiled nine albums of drawings and watercolour paintings, which comprise a unique view of a long vanished way of life and a seemingly immutable landscape.

A Royal commission was, apparently, something of a mixed blessing. It no doubt helped to further an artist's career, and it no doubt did something for his reputation, but it did not do a great deal for his pocket: the Queen is said not to have paid overmuch for the pictures she commissioned. She also knew quite precisely what she wanted, and the artists had to paint more or less to order. The ones who would not did not last long, and Charles Landseer, Sir Edwin's less famous brother, is a typical example. For the majority of those who know it, the mention of Sir Edwin Landseer's name will instantly evoke *The Monarch of the Glen*, or *The Stag At Bay*, which represent, perhaps, the pinnacle of this Victorian genre painting. The original of the latter is now in Dublin, but the inspiration is all around one in Glen Feshie.

Landseer had the ability to combine pathos with a touch of cruelty in his pictures, and he was very successful. He was one of Queen Victoria's favourites, and he visited Balmoral and other Royal estates on and off over a long period. The Queen, who was herself an accomplished watercolour painter, probably had lessons from him when at Balmoral. Landseer rather enjoyed the sporting life and, although a rotten shot, he neglected no opportunity for deer stalking, and similar pursuits. He certainly had a great fondness for the Highlands, where he could both indulge his tastes and soak up the atmosphere for his pictures. Glen Feshie was one of his favourite places, and he had a bothy, or summer cottage, here.

Seton Gordon, a great naturalist, author and photographer, once mentioned that a Landseer mural was still to be seen in the ruined chapel in the pinewoods beyond Glenfeshie Lodge. This was about fifty years ago. There is a mystery here because he was unlikely to make a mistake, but it is probable that what Gordon took to be a 'chapel' was, in fact, the ruin of Landseer's bothy. Now, only the chimney stack still stands, and if there was a mural on the chimney breast it is long gone. Landseer, like most Victorian landscape painters, made working drawings on the spot, using charcoal and pastels. These studies were used later, when permanent oil or watercolours were worked up in the studio. Landseer was known to try things out on the white plasered walls, and what Gordon saw was possibly the remnant of some working sketches – we shall never know. The only certainty is that Landseer worked here for several summers, and this walk is to the site of his highland home.

As in the previous walk, the most convenient start is from Achlean, and the route is followed past the waterfalls and down to the river by Achleum. From this point, follow the river upstream for about half a mile and cross the bridge to the other side. The river here thunders through a narrow defile, and it is worth lingering a little to enjoy the beauty and the fantasy of the natural sculptures in the water-worn rock. The little Scots pines by the roadside seem to be popular with crested tits. Carry on by the edge of the road for a mile or so to the next bridge. By the gate in the fence there is a notice about deer stalking: please heed it. It should be very obvious that the road is laid on the old – glacial – riverbed. The valley here is at least a mile wide, and it must once have been a magnificent stream, at least equal to the Spey. The hillside on the right often carries enormous herds of red deer stags, and the stunted pines by the road are often occupied by crested tits. At Carnachuin, by the Stalker's home, there is a simple memorial to members of the Fellcraft School, which was based here in the 1940s. This was a training school for potential officers, and there are many tales to be told of their activities in the district, both licit and otherwise. The view upstream is very grand, and is the main reason for choosing this side of the river.

Cross the bridge, and then pause by the cairn, which marks the boundary of the National Nature Reserve. It is quite usual to see groups of red deer hinds quietly grazing beyond the trees. When the wind is right it is not too difficult to get close enough for a photograph.

The track from here is obvious, and passes through some most attractive woodland to the bothy at Ruigh-Aiteachain. This is one of the better bothies, and its excellent state of preservation is no doubt due, in part, to its position. It still looks and feels much as bothies used to, but all too often now do not. Please remember that it is primarily a refuge and place of shelter, and bolt the door when you depart.

Near by, and a little upstream, there stands an isolated chimney stack. Solidly built in local stone, it has its back to the hill, and looks over a shallow depression to the river beyond. A trickle of ice cold and delicious water runs constantly from a little spring near by, and it is easy to imagine the idyllic life here in the summer time. The reality was probably rather different. The chimney stack is all that remains of Landseer's bothy, which is likely to have been similar to its slightly smaller and rougher neighbour.

Landseer never married, but he was far from averse to feminine company, and is supposed to have had a romantic attachment to the Duchess of Bedford, who owned the cottage he rented here in the glen. It is recorded that she was a frequent visitor during the sporting season. Sir Edwin and his aristocratic companion once were weather-bound here and found some time to experiment in the kitchen. The result was, apparently, 'Duchesse' potatoes – true or not, it makes a charming story.

Return to the bridge, but do not cross over to Carnachuin. Keep to the right bank, and follow the riverside track to the forest fence. The path through the forest emerges by Allt Garbhlach, and the ford is some way upstream. The track continues across rough country to Achleum. There is a lot of cover on this ground, so look out for deer, and also for uncommon birds. Ospreys and eagles hunt down this glen, and there are crested tits in the pines.

From Achleum the riverside path is followed back to Achlean. Note that Allt Fhearnagan will have to be forded because the bridge has been removed!

PART FOUR

Forests

AFTER THE LAST ice age a great boreal forest spread across the northern hemisphere and literally girdled the Earth. Enormous tracts of woodland still stretch across North America and Europe, but much of the old forest has disappeared from Britain, a victim of the need for clear ground for farming, and our apparently insatiable demand for softwood. Most of the large coniferous woodlands in Britain now are artificial, creations of the Forestry Commission and a few private owners, and they tend to consist of close-planted imported species of quick growing trees. Scotland has its share of this type of woodland, and 'tax-avoidance' planting has been rapidly increasing the area that is privately owned. The plantings have often produced a characteristic blanket woodland of spindly and barren trunks rising from an apparently lifeless understory, and whilst these woodlands may be commercially valuable, they are aesthetically dead.

It is fortunate that Scotland has also retained large areas of natural pine forest, which has been the native woodland for the past few thousand years. In a few remnants of the old pinewoods it is still possible to get an idea of how the country must have looked before the onset of man. The largest surviving areas are to be found in and about Badenoch and Strathspey, typically in the forests of Abernethy, Rothiemurchus, Glen More, Glen Feshie, and Glen Lui. Most of these old woods of Caledon have been worked commercially, on and off, for some four hundred years, and they no longer truly represent the wild country of long ago, but they do have an oddly primeval feel, and provide a real flavour of the past.

The Abernethy and Feshie forests are now owned and administered by conservation bodies and it may be expected that they will be allowed to return to something like the native forest of long ago. But deer are still a problem, and the methods used to protect young trees from their destructive browsing are bad for the local woodland birds. It would be better if the deer population could be reduced to about half its present level. Perhaps we should bring back the wolves?

Juniper, Scots pine and yew are the only three conifers now indigenous to Britain. Spruce was once a native tree, but it became extinct, and all the existing trees have been generated from imported stock. The old forest remnants consist mainly of native Scots pine and juniper, with thickets of birch and rowans, and some alder and willow scrub. The tree spacing varies, but it is nowhere very dense, and old trees usually lie and rot where they have fallen. In many areas the regeneration of the trees seems good, despite the deer, and there is also a large, rich and varied assortment of plants, animals, and insects in a deep and colourful understory that flourishes only where there is sufficient light.

The Scots pine is a most interesting tree, and is tremendously varied in appearance depending on its age. Young and immature trees are quite undistinguished, with greyish bark, dark green needles and a roughly conical shape. As such there is little to distinguish them from many other conifers. With maturity comes a contrast so great that the old trees might be easily mistaken for a different species. There is probably no more beautiful and majestic tree than a mature Scots pine, with its new bark shining like freshly etched and beaten copper in the bright sunshine of a spring day. These noble old trees display venerable age in every crack, crease, furrow and wrinkle of their lower trunks. Higher up, the new bark glows beneath large umbrellas of the darkest green, and these fragrant canopies provide a perfect foil for the yellow pollened spikes of the new cones.

Although 'forest' tends to evoke an area of woodland, there is another much older meaning of the word, and it crops up a lot in Scotland. Traditionally all land set aside for hunting deer and game is designated forest, and this includes the rough hill and moor country frequented by red deer. The forests of Upper Glen Avon, of Mar and of Gaick are all typical and local examples of this.

NOTE: A Government-funded working party spent some years examining the environmental problems of the area, and a Cairngorms Partnership Board co-ordinated the activities of the many interested bodies as preparations were completed for the area's designation as a National Park, which happened in 2003. One of their decisions was an intention to eradicate all alien tree species and re-generate the Caledonian forest locally as a 'Forest of Strathspey' and a 'Forest of Mar'. This had an immediate effect, and there has been wholesale felling of vast tracts of alien woodland in areas controlled by Forest Enterprise. The results are not pretty, but remember that the mess will diminish with time, and our grandchildren should be the beneficiaries. This may not be as simple as they think, and it is noticed with wry amusement that there is already vigorous regeneration of the alien conifers! Work is always in progress somewhere, and this can mean that a path or forest road on the map may be temporarily closed. This is for your safety.

The Visitor Centres know the current situation and will always offer advice if asked.

WALK 13

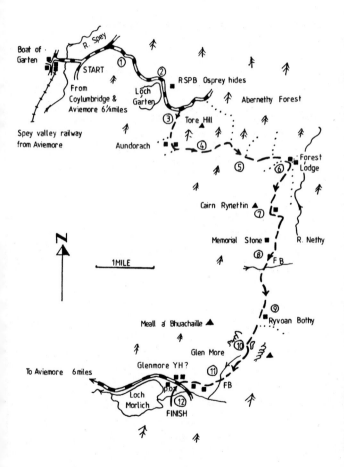

Boat of Garten

R. Spey

START

From Coylumbridge & Aviemore 6½miles

Spey valley railway from Aviemore

Loch Garten

RSPB Osprey hides

Abernethy Forest

Tore Hill

Aundorach

Forest Lodge

Cairn Rynettin

R. Nethy

Memorial Stone

FB

N

1MILE

Meall a' Bhuachaille

Ryvoan Bothy

Glen More

Glenmore YH?

To Aviemore 6 miles

Loch Morlich

FB

FINISH

Bird Watching about
Loch Garten

THIS IS NOT a circular walk, and transport will be required to the start at Loch Garten and from the finish in Glenmore. From Aviemore, follow the B970 road, turning to the left at Coylumbridge. About six miles beyond Coylumbridge, and after the Boat of Garten junction, there is a minor road to the right, and Loch Garten is about a mile down this road. It is the base for, perhaps, the best-known RSPB reserve in Britain, and is well sign-posted. Across the loch, the Kincardine Hills form the northern boundary of Glen More, and the walk back to there is about twelve miles.

Because it is all on forest tracks or roads, it could be a good idea to forget that this is a walking book, and hire a bicycle. Another option could be to travel from Aviemore to Boat of Garten on the Strathspey Railway, and either walk or cycle from there. The snags with the railway are the restricted operating days and the late start, but you may well consider that the considerable pleasure and nostalgia of travelling on one of the lovingly restored and maintained trains is adequate compensation. However, there are all sorts of possibilities – use the OS map and some imagination.

It is well known that Loch Garten is the home of the ospreys, which settled down here in the 1950s, after an absence of half a century. Many pairs have been reared since then, and in April each year they return to Strathspey to breed. The most famous site is down a track on the east side of the loch, and a special hide serves the burned and blasted pine, which is festooned with barbed wire for the protection of a pair of birds. There is adequate car parking, and there are some way-marked walks around the loch.

Carry on along the road, and turn right at the first junction, past the settlement of Aundorach and Torehill Cottage. At a left bend in the road, where a forestry road goes off to the right, turn southeast, down the forest road, and follow it, at first southeast, and then almost due east, until just short of Forest Lodge and the River Nethy. The whole of the woodland here is now owned and administered by the RSPB, and it is a veritable Paradise for bird watchers. The following list of local species is not at all exhaustive; it is merely an appetiser:

Black grouse, capercaillie, crested tit, siskin, crossbill, osprey, great spotted woodpecker, golden eagle, sparrowhawk.

Now turn right, almost due south, and follow the Ryvoan path past Rynettin, and out of the forest. The way goes by the Memorial Stone (to a young man killed in the 1914-18 war) and on past Ryvoan Bothy. There surely cannot be another mountain area with so many memorials and monuments in such a small compass. There are more than a dozen between Glen Feshie and Loch Pityoulish, and a visit to each would make for an interesting walking holiday – just a thought that is explored more thoroughly in a separate chapter.

From Ryvoan it is straight down the 'Yellow Brick Road' to Glenmore. This track was so dubbed by a walking companion many years ago, and the name seems particularly apt for this stony pink and yellow track. It is a way to and from the wilderness, just like the road in the once-popular song.

If time permits, take the track to the left, just after Ryvoan Bothy. After about half a mile there is a small pile of stones on the left, and a faint track leads down through the heather to some trees by a lochan. This is Loch a' Gharbh-choire, which is sometimes a breeding ground for black-headed gulls. The nests are usually on the tops of the stumps in the east end of the loch. This little loch is fished by a local osprey – see Walk 8.

WALK 14

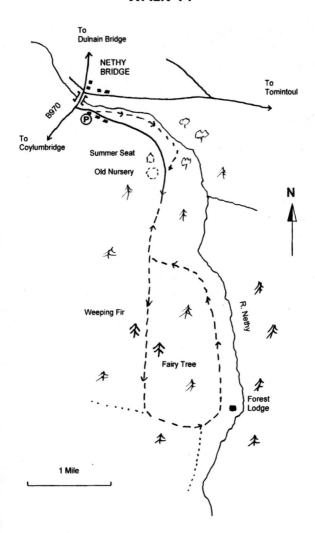

The Abernethy Woodlands

TWO HUNDRED AND fifty years ago Nethy Bridge was at the heart of the huge industrial complex of the York Buildings Company, and its HQ was at Coulnakyle, where there is now an imposing Adam house by the old farmstead. The woodlands all about would have reverberated to the sound of boring mills, saw mills, the foresters' axes and the noise of the iron smelters. It was an area of feverish activity that lasted for some twenty years between 1720-1740. Nowadays, modern housing occupies the industrial sites by the river, and there is virtually no tangible evidence to link the area to its early industrial past. The industrial heritage is represented by the relatively recent remains of the forestry industry of the last hundred years. Abernethy Forest is the largest remnant of the ancient Caledonian forest that once covered most of the Highlands, and the glorious mixed woodland that radiates from the village centre in Nethy Bridge provides scope for a seemingly endless series of interesting and enjoyable woodland walks.

Entering the village from the south, turn right immediately before the bridge and park at the Community Centre. Several woodland walks radiate from here, and one of the shortest and most attractive follows the Riverside Trail, which is signposted on the river bank immediately opposite the hall.

The path follows the river for about a mile, to the point where it joins Dell Road. It is a delightful stroll through old woodland, and in late spring the beauty of the masses of white blossom on the riverside bird cherries has to be seen to be believed. The riverside fields that open out to the right after a few hundred yards are also a picture, highlighted with banks of purple and yellow heartsease violets. The sight and scent of the trees, blossom and flowers, combined with the sound of the water and the birdsong, turn this riverside path into a little patch of earthly Paradise.

At the junction with Dell Road there are two options: turn right, and walk back down Dell Road to the village, or turn left, and carry on towards the Dell. This second is a much more interesting option, and leads past the Summer Seat – a fantastic Victorian summer house, said to use samples of all the different tree species in the forest. This stands on the left of the path, and overlooks the old nursery that was once used for raising trees from seed. Much further on, about two miles from the village, on the road to Forest Lodge, there are two quite remarkable Scots

The Fairy Tree

pines: a weeping fir, which is actually an extremely rare specimen of a weeping Scots pine, is on the right hand side of the path. A little further on, in a clearing on the opposite side of the way, the Fairy Tree is a magnificent ancient pine.

In about half a mile there is a 'T' junction, and the forest road should be followed to the left towards the old shooting lodge of Forest Lodge, which is a large Victorian building that is Grade II listed, and said to be the largest timber house in Scotland. The road is followed back to the north, to where it rejoins the Dell road at NJ014182. Turn right to go back to the village. The short walk by the river is about two miles, but the round trip excursion to Forest Lodge is at least ten miles, and needs a full day.

PART FIVE

Rothiemurchus

THE PARISH OF Rothiemurchus – the Plain of the Great Pines – covers a large area and encompasses a wide variety of countryside. The boundary runs along the Spey, from Aviemore to just beyond Loch an Eilein, and then turns to take in Glen Einich and the Sgorans, part of Braeriach and the Lairig Ghru, and the woodland towards Loch Morlich. It continues northwards to Loch Pityoulish.

To the ordinary visitor this will appear to be a wild, rugged, and (in some places) barren land, and the fact that much of it is farmed may seem a ludicrous idea. But farmed it is, and the range of produce is wide. Animal husbandry provides cattle, sheep, deer and trout; arable farming is carried on in the riverside haughs, and timber is cropped in the forest. The land is all privately owned, mainly by the Grants, who work in harmony with Scottish Natural Heritage, and the general public has been given very generous access. Much of the country is included in the National Nature Reserve and will be an important element in the new Cairngorms National Park.

There is a very special feel about this place, and one can enjoy a blissful solitude without feeling in any way alone. The red tracks of granite sand and pine needles wind between honeyed tussocks of russet heather. Junipers form prickly pillars in the grassy flats, their blue-bloomed berries redolent of resin and gin. Wood ants build their hills in a frenzy of activity that goes on forever, and the boulders lie everywhere, clothed with club moss and multi-coloured lichen. Through the pine trees, green-black in the bright sunshine, Carn Eilrig dominates the landscape out of all proportion to its modest height. Aloof and alone, it guards the entrances to Glen Einich and the Lairig Ghru.

Along these tracks one is walking on history, and the forest is crossed by the *Rathad nam Mearlaich* – the Thieves Road – which was used by the caterans of Lochaber on their forays into the fat cattle lands of Banff and Moray. Their route through Rothiemurchus was from the Feshie, by Loch an Eilein to Loch Morlich, then through Ryvoan and across the Nethy to Tomintoul. The MacGregors, from far away Balquhidder, who were also noted drovers and caterans, were said to have had a long association with the Rothiemurchus Grants. Seton Gordon records that the legendary Rob Roy MacGregor was said to have supported the Laird of Rothiemurchus during a bitter dispute with the Clan MacIntosh, when the MacIntoshes were threatening to burn the Doune. As a direct result of Rob Roy's intervention, the MacIntoshes were bested and the threat removed. Following this incident, two MacGregors were left behind to get help if needed, and one was given the tenancy of Aultdruie.

There are many versions of this story, but it is true that the MacGregors occupied the little farm until 1890, when Hamish MacGregor, the last farmer, died. It was probably a desirable holding then, but the ruined buildings in the river flats are now a mute reminder of the hard life in centuries past.

The estate is certainly ancient, and at the time of the Norman alliance with the old Scots, it is said to have belonged to the Norman family of Comyns. They fell out of favour, and in the 14th century Alexander Stewart, a bastard son of Robert II, acquired the estate. It then passed to the Shaws, and having been forfeited to the Crown – Scottish history is complicated – the right to the estate was purchased by the Grants, and about 1600 it was settled on Patrick, second son of the Clan's chief. It has remained in Grant hands since then, and the present laird is the thirteenth in direct succession.

Forest and Rothiemurchus are practically synonymous, and the area is always associated with woodland. But 'forest' is used here in the old sense to mean deer forest, which includes large tracts of open moor and hills. There is, of course, a great deal of wooded country, which is not Forestry Commission land, and it shows. Indeed, some of the finest remnants of the old birch and pine woodlands are found here, and are naturally regenerating, despite constant grazing by deer. As might be expected, this is a very good area for studying woodland creatures. Wildlife is abundant, and virtually any naturalist could spend a happy holiday entirely within the forest boundary.

WALK 15

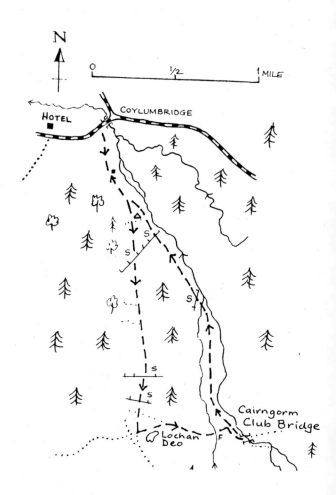

A Walk in the Forest

ALMOST OPPOSITE THE road end at Coylumbridge (NH915107) is the effective start, or finish, of the Lairig Ghru. It looks just like an unmade road, with a caravan site down by the river on the left, but this is an illusion because it is much more than that: it is the entrance to an enchanted world. Rothiemurchus is really quite incredible – it is just one of several remnants of the old boreal forest in this part of the world, and it is certainly the most accessible, yet it has as much impact, and more raw, primeval feel, than all the others put together. If you want to know what virgin pine forest is really like, then this 5-mile walk is for you.

Immediately through the gate there is a different world, and the transition from open country is abrupt. This is a mixed woodland, and roe deer could be grazing quite unseen on the right only a few yards from the track. Lairig Ghru Cottage on the left, once a cheerful and most photogenic log cabin, now ruined by fire, marks the end of civilisation until Braemar.

The landscape here is varied, and the dense and distinctly wild woodland to the right is in marked contrast to the cool green grassland down by the river. The rough track of cobbles and pink granite sand divides the two, and don't be afraid to deviate from the road and explore a little way along the animal tracks that lead off on either side. This is moth country, and entomologists come from far and wide to study these rare, but often rather drab, denizens of the pine woods.

In a little while the forest thins, and near a big cairn there is a parting of the ways. The track branches to the right, and it is marked for Glen Einich and Loch an Eilein. The woodland gives way to a rough but open scrubland of grass, heather, and various mosses, dotted here and there with junipers and a few trees, and the land rises a little towards the old farmstead of Whitewell. There is dense forest away to the right, and in the background the dark and dramatic cone of Carn Eilrig dominates the south, where it guards the entrances to Glen Einich and the Lairig Ghru.

The maze of tracks to left and right can be ignored, but back in the woodland, beyond the fence, and about two miles from the start, a major forest road cuts across to right and left (NH916079). This is a stretch of the ancient Rathad nam Mearlaich used by the Lochaber freebooters on their cattle rustling forays into the rich country to the east. Their route is now followed to the left, but pause a while at little Lochan Deo, tucked away on the right, and partly hidden, just by the junction of the roads.

The way goes now through increasingly splendid country to the river, which is reached at the Cairngorm Club Bridge. The original ford is close by the bridge, on the right, and it must have been a rough old crossing when the melt was flowing well. The water is delicious and is always icy cold. It is worthwhile going upstream a short distance to the confluence of the Druidh and Am Beanaidh. This is majestic country, but often harsh and wild: witness the testament of the fallen trees. These have been literally torn out by the roots, victims of some incredible and violent winter gales. Wind speeds of 172 mph were recorded on Cairngorm in 1987 – twice as violent as those that devastated the English woodlands!

Go back now to the junction about a quarter of a mile away, and take the branch of the Lairig Ghru track that follows the forest margin close by the river. The outward route is rejoined at the cairn, and the road is not then far away. Coylumbridge Hotel is just a couple of hundred yards down the road to Aviemore, and a dram, or a long, cool pint, or both, in Walkers, will provide a well deserved conclusion to the walk.

Have a look at the roadside below the pines in the hotel grounds. It is absolutely littered with the gnawed remnants of pine cones. This is the work of the many hungry red squirrels with which the area abounds. The 'pineapple' top is the giveaway – field mice eat the lot.

WALK 16

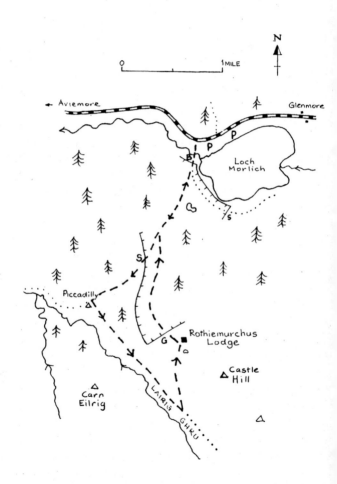

The Lairig Ghru

THE SHAPE OF the landscape in these highlands is mostly the result of glacial action. The mountains were sculpted and the valleys excavated by the relentless grinding of the ice. Frost, snow, wind and water continue the process, and the product is a wild and romantic countryside. A great ice-gouged valley runs north from Blair Atholl to its junction with the Dee at White Bridge near Braemar. The northwards continuation of the valley towards Aviemore is the Lairig Ghru, which transects the Cairngorms' highest peaks.

This walk, which is a round trip from Loch Morlich, goes to the pass and traverses some rugged but beautiful country. The scenery is varied and dramatic, the distance is about five miles, and the walk will take about three hours.

Take the B951 road out of Aviemore to the first picnic area and car park at the beginning of the loch (NH958097). Cross the Bailey bridge over the Luineag, and walk up the road towards Rothiemurchus Lodge. Follow the track to the right at the junction signposted for Piccadilly, and cross the deer fence at the stile with the dog flap by it. As the fence starts to bear off to the left it takes the new plantings with it, and the path goes ever more deeply into the old forest. The path starts to go quite steeply downhill, and just after this two sylvan glades open up to the left; tread lightly and quietly now, for the glades are a favourite haunt of deer. When the wind is southerly and there is no one else about it can be most rewarding in this spot. If a browsing roebuck senses an intruder and barks, bark back from cover, and wait. Roe deer are quite inquisitive, and he might come over for a closer look.

The track continues to a crossroads in the forest where there is a large National Nature Reserve cairn and, maybe, a sign pointing to Braemar. Piccadilly was, at one time, a most important junction. The Lairig track continued north to cross the Luineag by a pine-log bridge to Coylum Bridge and beyond, and a branch of the track, by the river, went east to the Medicine Well, *Fuaran Raoin Fhraoich*, (os *Rinraoich*), which drew visitors from as far afield as Braemar. The east-west road that crosses here is the Thieves Road. Apart from the road surface, the country here is probably little altered since those times, and it should be savoured, for this is the oldest, and the largest, and the least changed, remnant of the ancient natural woodlands of Britain. It is something to be cherished, and it is a privilege just to walk here.

Take the track south towards Braemar. The surrounding woodland becomes progressively more beautiful as the path ascends, and Carn Eilrig is prominent to the right, across the valley of the Allt Druidh. As the woodland starts to peter out the scenery all about is an assault on the senses, so theatrical are the views. Behind, below, and to the right, the river courses through a gorge clothed densely in variegated woodland. Ahead, the sheer-walled pass between the mountains beckons or threatens, depending on the weather.

This is the fringe of the forest, and as the path climbs higher onto the open moor the woodland clings to the shelter of the deeply cut valley sides. Across the valley, the east flanks of Carn Eilrig are often speckled with grazing deer. The general beauty of the place was recognised by those great artists the Ordnance Survey cartographers, and the old map of 'Aviemore and the Cairngorms' had a striking drawing of a cock caper-caillie against the background of a delightful and intriguing river valley. The viewpoint for this scene is about NH940067, just to the side of and below the path. A little way further on there are spectacular views to the south, over the massed gravel banks, relics of a long vanished glacial lake. Braeriach dominates the view to the right, and the dramatic cliffs of Lurcher's Crag soar above the valley on the left. The Lairig continues to the south, rising slowly through a crazy jumble of shattered rocks.

Just about where the woodland finally peters out, a track cuts in from the left. Bear left, away from the Lairig, and follow the path, which goes roughly north, across the flank of Castle Hill and up to Rothie-murchus Lodge, a recreation centre for Army personnel. The way from here, now on a gravel road, curves round to the left, and then goes strongly downhill, past Lochan nan Geadas, and back to the car park.

Wayfaring

EVEN IN THIS mountain wonderland it is possible to be stuck for something to do. The cloud may be down; the tops may have lost their appeal on a cold day, or it could be that the beach is 'out' on a sizzlingly hot day . . . whatever the reason, it just seems that nothing in particular appeals. This is the ideal time to try a spot of wayfaring. It has been described as orienteering without the sweat, and it is certainly a forest walk with a difference. Another advantage of wayfaring is its flexibility. The course can be tailored to suit one's exact requirements, from an hour's amble at one extreme, to a full and strenuous day in the forest at the other.

There is a wayfaring course in the Queen's Forest, and a cheap Wayfaring Package can be bought from many outlets in the area, including the Forest Enterprise Centre and the shop in Glenmore. The main components are an excellent map of the Queen's Forest, some general notes and information about wayfaring, and suggestions about how to get started. Equipped with this map and a compass it is possible to wander about in the forest without using any of the forest-walk paths. In fact, the basic pack provides all that is necessary for a wide variety of forest walks. If you really want to learn to read a map and use a compass, this is the ideal way to do it.

To give some sense of purpose go to the point

where the master map is displayed – this varies with the reafforestation programme; ask when purchasing the pack. The map has all the wayfaring controls marked on it. The controls are wooden posts with a distinctive symbol and code letters painted on the top, and the idea is to mark-up your own map with the locations and numbers, and then seek them out on the ground. Complete instructions come with the map. It is really orienteering, but a lot more relaxed.

It is not supposed to be competitive – that is normally a feature of orienteering – and wayfaring is an ideal basis for a fun family day out in the woods. If you go round the controls and keep a note, you can send off and get a diploma from the local Orienteering Club. It looks impressive.

It is a different world in the forest, and it isn't just a lot of trees. There are rare flowers and birds, dramatic ravines and secret lochans. There are no routes – you make your own – and there is a lot of quiet satisfaction and a real sense of achievement to be had in navigating from point to point in what is, after all, a quite bewildering terrain. Be prepared for funny looks from the ordinary walkers you will see from time to time as you burst out of the forest, cross one of the tracks, and disappear into the undergrowth on the other side. And if you dress discreetly and move quietly you could see a lot of unusual wildlife.

A most attractive and interesting alternative is to try one or more of the Pathfinder routes on the Rothie-murchus Estate. Pathfinding is essentially the same as wayfaring, but there are three different levels: the two and a half mile Scout, the five and a half mile Traveller, and the seven and a half mile Explorer. They all use the extensive network of paths and quiet roads within the boundaries of the estate, and cover an extensive, varied and fascinating range of countryside. At the time of writing the Forest Enterprise woodlands have been devastated by the clearance of alien trees, and are none too attractive, so the Pathfinder is the sensible option.

The Pathfinder pack can be purchased from the Visitor Centre at Inverdruie, where the master map is also to be found. Although somewhat more expensive than Forest Enterprise's Wayfaring pack, the Pathfinder set is well worth the extra money.

PART SIX

General Wade and the Military Roads

FIELD MARSHALL GEORGE Wade was, by any standards, a remarkable man. Born in Ireland in 1673, he entered the army and was an Ensign in the 10th Foot Earl of Bath's Regiment in 1690. He had risen to the rank of Captain by 1695. In 1702, as one of the Duke of Marlborough's officers, he distinguished himself at the siege of Liege when his grenadiers stormed and captured the citadel. His promotion was rapid, and by 1708 he was a Brigadier, second in command of an expedition to Menorca.

Menorca has a rough and mountainous terrain, and when Wade arrived, there were no roads. The expedition had great trouble with artillery transport, and Wade would have been quick to see that decent military roads were essential; he may have served his road-building apprenticeship here. In 1711 Wade was promoted to Major General, and he left to take command

General Wade

of the army in Ireland. It is almost certain that he gave a flying start to Richard Kane, Governor of Menorca from 1713 and famous, amongst other things, for his roads. When Wade retired from the army he became an MP, first for Hindon and then for Bath.

After the rebellion of 1715, the general disarmament of the Clans placed the many law-abiding Highlanders at the mercy of those few people who chose to live outside the law. The Jacobite cause rumbled on, and there was widespread discontent and many complaints and appeals to the King, especially from Simon Fraser, Lord Lovat. In 1724 Wade was brought out of retirement, recalled to the colours, and sent to Scotland to sort out the problems. He wasted no time, and on 10 December following he reported to the King on the general situation, and in particular commented on the need for adequate roads and bridges.

On 25 April 1725 Wade was appointed Commander-in-Chief of Scotland. Thus began a third and legendary career during which this formidable man formed the famous Black Watch regiment, and constructed a network of military roads and rebuilt the forts down the Great Glen. Wade's plan was to create a triangle of roads connecting the main forts in the Highlands, with access from the south along a road that is largely followed by the modern A9. The main route north was from Dunkeld to Fort George (Inverness). A secondary road was later made from Crieff via Aberfeldy. This joined the main road at Dalnacardoch, at the south end of Drumochter Pass, by the junction with the old Edendon/Gaick track to Ruthven. Wade's road from the south, through Crieff, Aberfeldy, and Trinafour still exists and is followed by modern minor roads. It provides a pleasant approach to Strathspey for those motorists who are not enslaved by the clock. It is also just about the shortest route from Stirling to Strathspey, which tells us a lot about Wade's surveyors.

Another road traversed the Great Glen along the east side of Loch Ness (now mainly A82, B852/862), and connected Fort William, Fort Augustus and Fort George. The final link, between Fort Augustus and the main north-south route, was built in 1732 on the line of the old drove road over the Corrieyairack Pass. Near to this junction, at Ruthven, Wade had renovated the old barracks in 1727 and added a stable block in 1734. This was part of his continuing policy of maintaining a strategic presence, whilst also providing decent and comfortable depots for his troops.

There was a touch of irony in the use of the military roads by Prince Charles Edward Stewart during the rebellion of 1745. Wade, by now a Field Marshall, was an inactive bystander in charge of an army at York as Charles campaigned into England, and finally retreated to defeat at Culloden at the hands of the butcher Cumberland. Making further use of Wade's roads, Prince Charles fled to France in 1746. Wade finally retired in 1748. In the years 1725-38 he had constructed over 240 miles of road and 30 bridges for not much more than £20,000. Equivalent to almost £0.5 million a mile at today's prices, the roads were quite a bargain.

The forts had no real effect, and they were either

ignored or destroyed by the Highlanders. But the roads
and bridges built by Wade and his successors opened
up the Highlands, and formed the basis for the roads
we use today. Many of our modern roads, such as the
A9, and the Lecht road to Grantown-on-Spey, largely
follow the lines of the roads created by Wade and his
successor, General Clayton. There are other stretches,
long since redundant and overgrown, that can be
followed as footpaths or hill tracks. Speyside has many
examples of these, and interested walkers will find some
fascinating and rewarding routes on the old Wade
roads. The two routes that follow illustrate the delightful variety and scenic contrast so typical of the general's
roads. The first is a gentle switchback of a road through
delightful woodland with picturesque river views. The
other route offers an inviting and invigorating stretch
of open moorland with high skies and hills on either
hand. Enjoy!

WALK 18

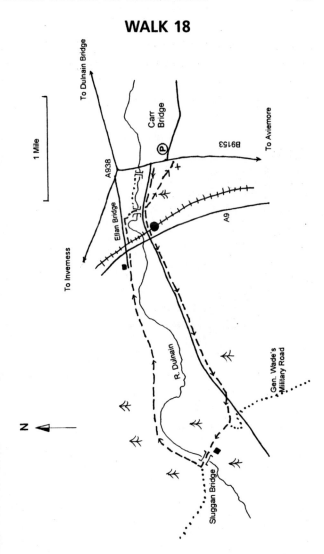

Sluggan Bridge and the Military Road

A CHARMING HIGHLAND village that sits happily by the river Dulnain, Carrbridge is a famous place in skiing circles. The first Scottish ski school was established here by the Austrian Klaus Fuchs, and the simple little monolith opposite Struan House Hotel commemorates his life and his achievements. The sport still flourishes in the winter months, and there is now a Nordic (crosscountry) ski school here as well. This peaceful little place is famous for the picturesque old bridge to which it owes its name, situated on an ancient corpse road to Duthill churchyard. It was built by the Earl of Seafield in 1717 to ease the passage of funeral parties across the Dulnain river. The bridge, which was probably not used by pack horses, was badly damaged by floods shortly after it was built. It is often supposed that the bridge was built by General Wade, but this is not the case, as Wade was still an MP in England when this arch was made. The steps on the green by the bridge lead to a viewing point, and the prospect is pictured in many publications. It is an exquisite scene.

A Wade bridge was built in 1728, at Sluggan, on the old military road to Inverness, and one can only speculate about the reaction of the locals at that time to the invasion of their village by the licentious soldiery that was building the road. A verse of W H Auden's might just sum it up:

> O what is that sound which so thrills the ear
> Down in the valley, drumming, drumming?
> Only the scarlet soldiers, dear,
> The soldiers coming.

Sluggan bridge is the objective for this pleasant half-day walk. Park in the large car park near the school in the centre of Carrbridge. Go right on the main street then walk up the little by-road to the left, sign-posted for the station. The road is metalled, but once past the station there is a pleasant grassy verge to walk on, and the scenery is a constant delight with heather moorland, woods and fields alternating on either hand.

Two and a half miles from Carrbridge, in the woods, about half a mile beyond the cattle grid (NH875213), a track to the left, coming downhill from the south and as straight as an arrow's flight, is the old military road from Dunkeld to Inverness. Its continuation through the gate to the right is the way to Sluggan bridge. A little way into the wood the road swings sharply to the left and the bridge can be seen, far below and far away to the right, at the bottom of the valley. Wade's old road plunges steeply down through a sharp hairpin bend towards the river, and it passes through a fine old mixed woodland of birch and Scots pine. It can be a bit wet here at times, but it is always easy to proceed dry shod. There is a rich understory, and many seedling trees, ant hills and foraging wood ants. The woods are alive with the sound of birdsong, and this woodland is also a haunt of capercaillies. In spring they often can be heard objecting to the walker's presence with a rather bad-tempered and guttural gobbling. As the road approaches the ruined farmstead of Sluggan the woods give way to rough pasture, and the bridge is straight ahead.

Sluggan is the Gaelic name for a throat or gullet, and it will be seen that it is very apt just here. The valley closes in upstream, and there are steep banks on both sides of the river. The approach to the bridge is bounded by odd clumps of trees: larch, birch and bird cherry, with an occasional rowan, and it is all so incredibly colourful in the autumn. The bridge crosses the stream in a great soaring single arch above the white shingle but, although typical of his style, the existing bridge is not the work of Wade. It is a Telford-built replacement for the original, which was badly damaged or swept away with many other bridges in the region during the great flood of 1829. After a long period of dilapidation the bridge has been repaired and the parapets have been replaced, and it now serves the SUSTRANS cycle network – what a good idea to use one of the original highland roads for this purpose – so do not be surprised to encounter cyclists.

Over the bridge the old road goes on towards Slochd and Inverness. The path back to Carrbridge is to the right, through more woodland. Cross the bridge and go right immediately beyond the tumbled ruins of an old building. A faint but definite track passes first through birch woods, and then through pasture and rough farmland high above the river to its continuation as a minor road at Dalrachny Beag. Walk along this road to a point about 50 yards past the entrance to Wolf Lodge where, opposite some timber fencing, an iron gate opens onto a footpath down to the elegant metal structure which is Ellan foot bridge. There is now a choice to be made: the track to the left is a delightful walk through mixed woodland by the riverside back into Carrbridge; alternatively, cross the bridge and follow the path through the Trekking Centre field and then up Urquart's Brae to the road near the station. Please leave all gates as you find them. From here either go left down the road, or else enter Ellan Wood on the other side of the road and take the path through the woods, going east past the cemetery, and back into the village.

WALK 19

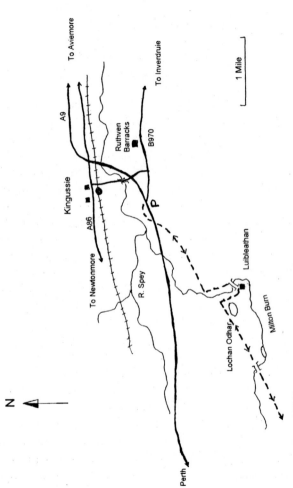

Luibleathan and the Dunkeld Road

THE OLD MILITARY roads in the vicinity of Aviemore are very fragmented, and many of the lines are difficult to follow because they are hidden within tracts of modern forest. They look very much like modern forest rides, and are not really worth walking. There are, however, some notable exceptions like this section of the old road from Dunkeld to Inverness, which crossed the Spey using a ferry in the vicinity of Ruthven Barracks. The Barracks – which were probably a major staging point for the army on the old military road – still stand, although they are somewhat ruinous having been blown up by the Jacobites in 1746. The majority of travellers do not come this way nowadays: they pass by unheeding, and at great speed, on the nearby A9. Although the old road is no longer a highway, it is a delectable walking route in a little visited part of Strathspey, and this short walk follows the road to the south to the old house of Luibleathan – the name signifies a broad loop in a stream.

Drive out of Kingussie on the B970, sign-posted for Ruthven Barracks. Cross over the river and, at the top of the rise, where the road swings sharply left, take the cul-de-sac to the right by the old farmstead and follow the rutted and pot-holed road, built on the foundation of Wade's old road, for about a quarter of a mile. You will reach a parking place for two or three cars by the tunnel under the modern A9. Walk through the tunnel and go off to the left, uphill, to the side of the A9. Carefully cross the modern road and go through the gate diagonally opposite. A track goes off from here, slightly uphill and heading virtually due southwest. As the rise is breasted the old military road is evident as a broad track, with banks on either side, running as straight as a die into the distance.

This is a wonderful stretch of country, and the road undulates slightly as it maintains a generally level course over the heathery grassland. There are low rolling hills to the left and right, the sky seems very high, and the mountains seem very far away on each side of this broad plain. Away to the right, in the far distance, tiny ant-like vehicles can be seen moving slowly on the modern road, but nothing can detract from the pleasure of walking here.

The track passes through a modern conifer plantation – please leave the gates as you find them – and then, a little further on, a grassy mound on the right, with tumbled stones and the remains of what appear to be old field walls, are all that is left of the Milehouse of Nuide. This was an inn on the old road but, like the travellers, it is long gone. There is the odd wind-blasted tree and, a sure sign of past habitation, plentiful nettles. There are also masses of mountain pansies (*Viola lutea*), and their delicate purple and yellow flowers are a delight in the short grass in late spring and early summer. Further on, an easily forded stream has the remains of old bridge abutments, but the bridge was used for building stone a long time ago.

About two miles from the start, Milton Burn is not easily forded. There never was a bridge here, but modern drainage of the moor has increased the water flow, and the sensible course nowadays is to follow the stream to the left, along a somewhat muddy track, to the old cottage of Luibleathan. The name means broad loop, which is what the burn makes through the moor just here. There is a wooden bridge close to the house, and this often has a greasy looking mess on the ends of the footway. Tread carefully because this is the territorial marking spraint of an otter. These attractive beasts are fairly common about here but, being nocturnal, they are most unlikely to be seen. The stream itself is a delight, and the little shrubs by the water are actually fairly mature dwarfed alders.

A track from the house rejoins the old road by Lochan Odhar, which is a very good spot for watching wildfowl, and there are usually a number of fowlers' hides on the shore. The ironwork of the fences and gates about here represents Victorian blacksmith work at its best, and is worth more than a cursory glance. The road may be followed for about a further mile to where another very well preserved Wade bridge will be found, just beyond a delightfully remote and reedy small lochan, which is over the rise on the left at NN726962. An eagle nests in the vicinity, so keep an eye on the sky about here. The road carries on, and provides some memorable and exhilarating walking for about six miles in all, all the way to Ettridge, near to the Falls of Truim. In fact, if two cars are available, it is a good idea to seek permission to leave a car near to the farm at NN685928, and park the other by the A9 tunnel at NN758993 and walk the whole stretch of road.

About a mile beyond the bridge, by the beginning of some birch woods, another burn is crossed. There is a shallow depression with embankments, but the bridge has gone. Loch Phones (pronounced Foness), on the right, heralds the approach to the shooting lodge of Phones House, which is an idyllic setting of green fields and birchwoods with low hills on either hand. After the House, the road is very well maintained all the way to Ettridge Lodge. Loch Ettridge is noted for its waterfowl. Beyond the lodge the road deteriorates and runs downhill to where it merges into the A9. Having walked this far it is worth crossing the A9 and walking a little way up the branch track to Crubenbeg to have a look at the Falls of Truim. Whatever the weather, and whatever option is chosen – a short excursion to Lochan Odhar, or beyond, and a return by the same route; or a longer linear walk from Ettridge to Ruthven, with the prevailing wind and the sun behind – a splendid walk is guaranteed. But it can be a bit exposed if the weather is cold, so be warned, and dress accordingly.

WALK 20

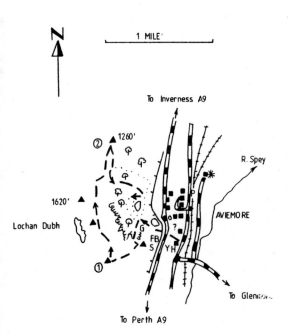

NOTE: The A9 footbridge is actually an underpass.

Craigellachie Nature Reserve

AT SOME TIME during any holiday there is a pressing need to go shopping. It may be that presents and post-cards have to be bought, or a map, or some new items of gear are required, and it must be admitted that, from time to time, it is nice to get away from the rigours of the hills. This walk provides an opportunity to do all these things without in any way compromising the idea and the spirit of a walking holiday.

Craigellachie is the well-wooded low hill with the sheer and craggy rock-face that provides such an impressive natural setting for the Aviemore Highland Resort. It is this rock, and not the fishing town in lower Strathspey, that figures in the Grant motto: 'Stand fast Craigellachie'. That Craigellachie endures is beyond doubt, and it is central to the little National Nature Reserve, which covers about two square miles of delectable low hill country to the west of Aviemore.

The reserve is notable on many counts, one of which is a resident pair of peregrine falcons. The reserve has a large area of birch scrub which is a habitat for many species of birds uncommon elsewhere in the area, for some reptiles and small mammals which are common but rarely seen, and for a variety of insect life that would be unusual anywhere, and which attracts naturalists from everywhere. The birch also plays host to an unusual bracket fungus – *Fomes fomentarius* – which occurs at only one other site in Britain.

Go to the Tourist Information Centre in Aviemore and see if they can still supply a leaflet describing the reserve, then go and have a cup of coffee while you read the leaflet. After the coffee it will be time to go to the reserve, which is approached through a corrugated iron tunnel under the A9.

It is strange that an area so delightful in itself is not overrun with other visitors. Not least of the delights of time spent here is that one rarely sees many other people. It is a little haven on the edge of the town, and most of the visitors encountered here seem to be specialist ornithologists, or other naturalists. This isolation is probably due to a combination of things, like the A9, which separates it from the town, general ignorance of the access tunnel's whereabouts, and lack of publicity.

Two paths lead to the tunnel, which was provided as the only access point when the A9 by-passed the town some years ago. One path runs from the main street, from a point between the youth hostel and a caravan site (NH894118). The other path starts from a bend in a road on the Highland Resort, near to the hotel (NH893123). It goes across the grass, following the fence, and picks up the other path near to the tunnel.

Once through the tunnel, go off to the right and follow the path to the left and up onto the duck-board staging, keeping to the higher level way. Near the first bend look for, and follow, a faint track that doubles back and goes uphill steeply through the woods to the left. This leads into a steep and narrow gully that goes straight up onto the ridge. It is easy scrambling all the way, but very rough and sweaty.

If this sort of scramble does not appeal, then carry on along the long, upper trail to where it meets a track which comes steeply downhill from the left, and obviously off the ridge. Follow this track up to the ridge, and then go left to the summit. At the top, the summit cairn is to the left, and this is the start of a pleasant little ridge walk offering superb views of the Cairngorms and this section of Strathspey.

At the end of the ridge, the path described above goes down to the nature trail and leads to some pretty rock and woodland scenery and a pleasant artificial lochan. The woodland is mainly birch scrub, which makes a pleasant change from the seemingly ubiquitous conifers elsewhere. There are many different butterflies and a riot of wildflowers, some of them very rare, and there are stoats and a lot of lizards. It is worthwhile going round the rest of the nature trail, using the leaflet obtained at the Information Centre.

Various walks are possible in the reserve, and some are shown on the map. You will soon create your own favourites, but the easiest course on a first visit is probably to follow a clockwise route around the nature trail on the finely graded path. This is constructed of gravel, stone slabs and duck-boarding, depending on the terrain. It is beautifully done and maintained, and the 'viewpoints' are well chosen. There is nothing here of the artificiality so often evident on other nature trails. No numbered posts and set pieces, and apart from the path, it is all as nature made it.

PLEASE DO NOT GO UP ONTO THE RIDGE IN APRIL AND JULY. These are critical months for the nesting peregrines, and they should be left undisturbed. During these two months there will be plenty of interest elsewhere in the reserve, and many opportunities to observe these magnificent birds from the best vantage point, which is at the foot of the crag. It is not unusual to see the parents teaching the young to hunt, and the sight of two peregrines, one with an adder wriggling in its beak, is one never to be forgotten.

Autumn is a particularly splendid season, and the reserve is especially beautiful then as the yellowing leaves – when sunlit – provide a green, grey and gilded tapestry that is a vivid and unforgettable backdrop to the town. The quiet and contemplative stroller here will be rewarded with the sight and sounds of many unusual birds, moths, small animals and plants. It is all the more attractive for the marked contrast with the great pine forests nearby. Wander and wonder, and haste ye back!

This is a very easy day, and at the end there will be time to go into Aviemore, or to Inverdruie and Coylumbridge, for a swim and some shopping before tea.

Monuments and Memorials

THE CAIRNGORMS ARE unique in many ways. It is well known that a combination of geology and climate has ensured that no other mountains have their particular attributes. But there is another aspect of this part of the Grampians that is, at least, unusual. There is no modern counterpart in any of the other mountainous regions of Britain, yet it seems not to have been remarked upon as a whole. The oddity is the sheer quantity and variety of memorials which, in some places, seem literally to litter the landscape. This is a comment, not a complaint. It must be said that, in general, the monoliths, obelisks, steles and other stones that some people have erected – usually as memorials to other people, who were only rarely locals – are never incongruous, and they usually blend quite naturally into the hillsides or woodlands which they adorn.

Some of the memorials are natural and not man-made. These are the stones, sometimes glacial erratics, which are so large or so prominent that they have been given a particular identifying name, as is the Gaelic way. Clach Mhic Cailein – the Argyll Stone of the Sgorrans – is a typical example. In other cases a natural stone has been transported and embroidered for a particular purpose – such is the Norwegian Stone of Glenmore. There are more.

The following list gives the names and OS map references of a baker's dozen or so of the district's many monuments and memorials:

The memorial at Rynettin (NJ012138) is a white granite stone on a knoll just to the west of the road. It is dedicated to one James Hamilton Maxwell, a young man from Edinburgh who was killed at Ypres during the Great War of 1914-1918.

Close to the Cairngorm Club bridge, in Rothiemurchus (NH926079), a pink granite stone commemorates a casualty of a 'v1' flying bomb attack on London in 1943.

At the Loch an Eileian branch on the Feshiebridge Road (NH891097) there is an elaborate monument to Dr Martineau, who once spent his summers at Polchar, close by. He was a Victorian clergyman and, like many churchmen of his time, he did not confine his activities to the Church. He founded a local library and a craft school, and he also secured general public access to much of the local forest; no mean achievement in those days. His sister Harriet was an equally formidable Victorian lady. In her day she was a famous writer of improving tales, but she is now chiefly remembered for an excellent guide to the English Lake District.

The Norwegian Stone in Glenmore (NH976098) is a memorial to the members of Kompani Linge, the Norwegian Commandos who carried out the Telemark Raid during the Second World War – see Walk 7.

In Glen More, by the stream that runs through the forest, and up a track beside an excavated drumlin, there is a cluster of tombstones on a knoll (NH987092). It is a late 19th century cemetery for the dogs of the Deniston family, then resident at the old Glenmore Lodge – the present youth hostel.

At the foot of Tor Alvie (NH869077), amongst the birches of Kinrara and just across the river from Inchriach, a simple granite obelisk is dedicated to the memory of Jane, Duchess of Gordon, in the reign of King George III.

On top of Tor Alvie (NH878089), the last Duke of Gordon has a splendid pillar as his personal monument.

Close by, still on top of Tor Alvie (NH873086), there is a Waterloo Cairn. It is a reminder of the battle, not the station!

Back across the Spey, near the west end of Loch an Eilein (NH898078), yet another granite slab is a memorial for General Rice. This poor soul met *his* Waterloo when he fell through the ice and drowned whilst ice skating on Boxing Day in 1892.

Kennapole Hill, which rises from the west end of the loch, is crowned by a cairn which commemorates a Duchess of Bedford (NH886071).

On Creag Dhubh, on the run up to the Sgorans, south of Loch an Eilein and to the west of the Glen Einich track (NH905040), is Clach Mhic Cailein – the Argyll Stone – a granite lump from which the eponymous Earl is said to have seen the mountains of Argyll when fleeing from his defeat in Glen Livet in 1594. It is probable that he came this way, and as Cruachan Ben can be seen from Carn Ban Mor, there may be more than legend to the name.

About half a mile to the south, on the same stony ridge (NH903034), another tor is sometimes called the Atholl Stone.

In a field by the private entrance drive to Dunachton

Lodge, at NH821046, there is a Pictish stone with a delicate carving of a roe deer's head.

Down the Feshie, just by the bridge at Carnachuin (NN846939), there is a memorial to members of the Highland Fieldcraft Training Centre, founded by Lord Rowallen as a training cadre for potential officers during the war of 1939 to 1945. It was a forerunner of the modern 'Outward Bound' schools.

When all else palls, or simply if the fancy takes one, a short walk can be based on a visit to any one of these artefacts. The 1:25,000 map is ideal for route planning. Don't forget to take a camera!

Natural History Notes

THE COUNTRYSIDE OF the Cairngorms area provides a wide variety of habitats, each of which has its own distinctive population, and these notes do not pretend to be anything other than a cursory comment on the unusual. The natural history of the region is the subject of a classic work – *The Cairngorms* by Adam Watson (Scottish Mountaineering Club & Trust, 1986) – that should be read by all those with more than just a passing interest in the area. The Forestry Commission guide to Glenmore Forest Park, which contains a wealth of related information, is also still in print, and both books are remarkably cheap. Many other books offer information about the locality and its inhabitants, and a few offer advice on how to observe them. As with many other things, an ounce of practice is worth a ton of theory, and the best thing is to go for a quiet walk and start looking.

It would be most unusual to spend any time in the hills and not come across some red deer. Fences exclude them from much of the woodland, but they are often seen in Glen Feshie, occasionally seen in Rothiemurchus near Piccadilly, in the plantations near Badaguish, and in the woodland between Glenmore and the funicular. In the early morning – about 6 a.m. – groups are often to be seen grazing around the caravans and tents on the campsite in Glenmore. The opposite sexes live separate lives throughout most of the year and come together only in the breeding season, about October.

Roe deer live in small family groups, and are wholly creatures of the woodland. They are very common in this area, and they do a good deal of damage to seedling trees.

Reindeer are different in every way. Originally resident here in ancient times, they became extinct along with the wild boars and the wolves. Mr Mikel Utse, a Sami from Sweden, visited Aviemore in 1947 and decided that it was reindeer country. He won a long battle against the bureaucrats and introduced the first beasts about 1952.

After a series of reverses the animals have settled down, and their number is increasing. Each day, the owner takes parties of visitors to a herd pastured near Glenmore, and brief acquaintance will show why they are so beloved by the Sami people. Normally they are delightfully friendly and gentle beasts, and they seem to like the company of people. But do be careful if you meet them on the hills: the bulls can be quite ferocious during the autumn rut, and paired animals, like Garbo, just want to be left alone.

A wild cat is not a domestic tabby gone wrong; it is a distinctive and very handsome breed of cat that is well established in Glenmore and Rothiemurchus. They are nocturnal and shy, and unlikely to be seen other than by accident, or during a visit to the Wildlife Park at Kincraig.

Blue, or mountain, hares are smaller than their lowland cousins, and they assume a white coat for the winter. They seem to be quite rare now, but have been seen above the Ryvoan pass, near Lochan na Beinne, over on the Bynacks, and on the Monadhliath moors behind Newtonmore.

The haggis is a wild creature also to be found wandering the remoter parts of Scotland, or so they say. . . *The haggis is a creature of the hills. A little furry animal with long legs, and a long nose and tail, it avoids people and is common only on the heathery slopes of the lower Cairngorms and the uttermost Braes of Glenlivet. It is similar in many ways to the largely aquatic desmans of Russia and the Pyrennes, and it may have evolved from animals brought here as a food source by Bronze Age beaker people, in much the same way that the Romans introduced the dormouse. The Scottish haggis (Haggis terrestis sinistrorsis scoti) is a sub-species of the type. It has the left legs slightly shorter than the right, which enables the animal to stand upright when progressing, as it normally does, anti-clockwise round the hill. The hunting season starts in December, and the usual method is to beat the hillside in a clockwise direction. The animals turn to escape, topple over, and roll to the bottom of the hill, where they are picked up by haggis baggers. A great delicacy, haggis is hung for a week, and is then skinned and boiled. Haggis is traditionally eaten on 25th January, accompanied by potatoes, turnips, whisky and bagpipe music.*

The pine marten, despite its name, is happy to live in any sort of woodland. Superficially like a polecat, it is larger, and has a white throat patch. A nocturnal hunter, it is unlikely to be seen, although it is not uncommon in the Speyside woods. Pine martens can become quite tame and one family, hooked on cake, regularly visits a Boat of Garten garden for a midnight feast.

Virtually extinct in other parts of Britain, red squirrels seem to be thriving here. They are common in all the woodlands, and their presence is indicated by the pine cone cores that litter the ground beneath their feeding places. At the café and shop in Glenmore, Bill Wilson has created a feeding area for the squirrels, and it is easy to pass a pleasant hour or so sitting in the café with a cuppa, watching the antics of the animals and birds outside.

Otters are not uncommon in Scotland but, being mainly nocturnal, they are rarely seen. They are certainly present in the streams about the old Wade road south of Ruthven, but most visitors will see only their territorial spraints on the ends of the footbridges, or on prominent boulders on the banks of the streams. The spraint looks a bit like tar or cat mess, and has a sweetish, musky odour. The best place to see these delightful creatures is at the Wildlife Park at Kincraig.

The variety and number of birds are enormous, but luck must play a part in the sighting of the rarities. The capercaillie is a large and ungainly bird that does not seem to fly well. It is more likely to be heard than seen, and in flight it looks like a black or brown turkey (the hens are brown). Rothiemurchus, near Piccadilly, and An Sluggan, near Badaguish, are known habitats. Blackcock were common many years ago, but now seem to be rare. They like to inhabit the country at forest margins, where old woodland gives way to pasture. Modern forestry and the spread of new plantations have reduced the area of this type of habitat, and this may be a reason for their decline. Abernethy and the west end of the Queen's Forest, around An Sluggan, seem to be localities where they might still be found.

Crossbills, tree creepers, long tailed and crested tits, siskins and woodpeckers may all be observed in the woods, and it is impossible to ignore the chaffinches, which flock around the clearings and in the car parks. A little patience and some crumbs should ensure some delightful photographs. Some ornithologists maintain that the local birds have their own particular dialect.

Away from the woods, red grouse live on the lower hills, and ptarmigan occur above 3,000 feet. Their nests are just scrapes in the ground, usually on the lee side of a rock. Golden eagles may be seen sometimes above Strath Nethy, the Lairig Ghru and down the Feshie, but people disturb them, and they may be deserting the area now that it is becoming so popular. Dotterel may be seen on Cairngorm plateau above the head of Loch Avon.

At Craigellachie, behind the Aviemore Centre, there is one of the most consistently successful peregrine breeding sites in Britain, and it is comparatively easy to enjoy the thrilling and rewarding sight of one of these marvellous falcons in flight, perhaps returning with a kill. Many people travel long distances to see these birds, and it was a surprise to learn recently that Britain now has one of the major populations. It is said, for instance, that only seventy are left in the whole of France.

For many visitors the great attraction now is the

ospreys, which sometimes seem to be everywhere. It may be a premature speculation, but their population seems to be increasing quite quickly, and sightings are commonplace in certain areas. At least one pair of birds is resident near Loch Morlich, and often can be seen fishing the loch. They are from a local nest which has been used, on and off, for some forty years. Five ospreys – two pairs and a loner – have been observed apparently fighting for possession of this nest. All very exciting. Another osprey, with a liking for Loch a' Gharbh-choire, probably spends the summer in the Braes of Abernethy. This area has now been bought by the RSPB, so its future may be secure.

The plant life of the region is as varied as the terrain, and uncommon varieties at low level include lousewort, chickweed-wintergreen, twinflower, butterwort and sundews. Cow, crow, and cloudberries, creeping azalea, alpine lady's mantle, saxifrages, moss campion, and a positively bewildering array of mosses and lichens may all be found at higher altitudes.

The local woodlands are a veritable paradise for entomologists, and they contain a wealth of moths, mosquitoes, midges, gnats, flies, mites, beetles, bugs, spiders, centipedes, millipedes, ants, and a whole host of weird and wonderful insects, many of them rare, and many of them to be found nowhere else. A famous naturalist was once asked if his life's work had taught him anything about God. 'Yes,' he is said to have replied, 'He is inordinately fond of beetles!' In the woodlands of Strathspey one can see the point. Superficially the forest floor is virtually dead, and nothing much stirs on the surface other than ants, and ground, dung, tiger and rove beetles. But lift the litter a little and it is a totally different world: a savage and violent jungle, where 'eat or be eaten' is the rule.

Wood ants' nests cannot be ignored, and these remarkable mounds of millions of pine needles house vast numbers of these busy creatures. Some of the nests are incredibly old: please do not disturb them, it could do irreparable harm. Most people seem to actively dislike insects, and dismiss them all as 'creepy crawlies', which is sad, for they are all interesting animals. One may, perhaps, make an exception in the case of midges, which are very irritating, in both meanings of the word. They are normally only of interest to anglers, fish, birds and bats, and are an unmitigated and uncontrollable nuisance to just about everybody else.

Gaelic Glossary

GAELIC PLACE NAMES tend to relate to the appearances or associations of things. This laudable and useful practice means that an elementary knowledge of the meaning of some words can add greatly to the information to be derived from a map. For example, *Coire an Lochain* is a rocky hollow with a small lake – an exact, economical, and useful description.

This is not the only benefit, but it does mean that there is no need for us to bother here about pronunciation, the rules for which are complicated, to say the least.

Aber, abar, obar – River estuary

Abhainn, avon (pron. arn) – River

Allt, ald, ault – Burn (Stream)

Aonach – Ridge, moor

Airgead, argiod – Silver

Aviemore – Great slope

Badaguish (pron. badwish) – Clump of pine trees

Badan Mosach – A nasty little clump of trees

Ban – White

Beag – Little

Bealach – Pass

Beinn, ben – Mountain

Beith – Birch tree

Buachaille, buchaille (pron. buckle) – Shepherd

Bidean – Pinnacle

Bodach – Old man

Brae – Slope

Buidhe (pron. bwee(th)) – Yellow

Caber – Tree

Cas – Steep

Chalamain – Pigeons

Chait – Cat

Ciste – Box

Clach – Stone, boulder

Cnap – Hillock, knob

Coire, choire (pron. corry) – Rocky hollow

Creag – Cliff, crag

Darroch – Oak tree

Dearg (pron. jarrag) – Red
Doire – Grove, hollow
Druidh (pron. drewy) – Shieling
Druim – Ridge
Dubh – Black
Eag – Notch
Eagach – Notched
Eas – Waterfall
Eilein – Island
Eilrig – Deer pasture
Fiacaill (pron. fyckle) – Teeth
Frithe (pron. free) – Forest
Gall – Foreigners
Gabhar, ghobhar (pron. gower) – Goat
Garbh – Rough
Geadas – Pike
Ghru – Grey
Gleann – Glen, narrow valley
Gorm – Blue, green
Gowrie – Goats
Inbher, inver – River bank
Iolaire – Eagle
Lairig – Pass
Laoigh – Calves (as in cows, not legs)
Leth-choin – Half dog
Liath – Grey
Linne – Pool

Lochan – Small lake
Loistge – Burnt
Luineag – Surging
Mam – Rounded hill
Meall – Hump, knob
Mhadaidh (pron. vatee) – Fox
Mheadhonach (pron. veeanach) – Middle
Moine – Mossland
Monadh – Mountains, moor
Mor, mhor – Great, big
Odhar – Drab, dappled
Ord – Steep hill
Rathad – Road
Riach, briach – Brindled
Ruadh – Reddish coloured
Ruadha – Promonotory
Sgorr, sgur – Sharp peak
Sluggan – Gullet
Sneachda (pron. snecta) – Snowy
Sron – Point, nose, ridge
Stac – Steep rock
Stob – Point
Strath – Wide fertile valley
Tom – Mound, knoll
Toul (pron. towl) – Barn
Uaine (pron. wain) – Green
Uisge (pron. ushga) – Water

Luath Press Limited

committed to publishing well written books worth reading

LUATH PRESS takes its name from Robert Burns, whose little collie Luath (*Gael.*, swift or nimble) tripped up Jean Armour at a wedding and gave him the chance to speak to the woman who was to be his wife and the abiding love of his life. Burns called one of *The Twa Dogs* Luath after Cuchullin's hunting dog in *Ossian's Fingal*. Luath Press was established in 1981 in the heart of Burns country, and is now based a few steps up the road from Burns' first lodgings on Edinburgh's Royal Mile.
Luath offers you distinctive writing with a hint of unexpected pleasures.

Most bookshops in the UK, the US, Canada, Australia, New Zealand and parts of Europe either carry our books in stock or can order them for you. To order direct from us, please send a £sterling cheque, postal order, international money order or your credit card details (number, address of cardholder and expiry date) to us at the address below. Please add post and packing as follows: UK – £1.00 per delivery address; overseas surface mail – £2.50 per delivery address; overseas airmail – £3.50 for the first book to each delivery address, plus £1.00 for each additional book by airmail to the same address. If your order is a gift, we will happily enclose your card or message at no extra charge.

Luath Press Limited
543/2 Castlehill
The Royal Mile
Edinburgh EH1 2ND
Scotland
Telephone: 0131 225 4326 (24 hours)
Fax: 0131 225 4324
email: gavin.macdougall@luath.co.uk
Website: www.luath.co.uk

Short Walks on Skye

Joanna Young
ISBN 1 84282 065 6 PBK £4.99

You don't have to be a fitness fanatic or a serious hiker to experience the beauty and wonders that the Isle of Skye has to offer. There are few other places in Britain that can offer such a wealth of short walks in places of such outstanding natural beauty.

This book describes forty short walks on Skye, the shortest of which is only a couple of minutes, the longest no more than 35. These excursions will take you to some of Skye's most magical places: beaches, rivers, woodlands, churchyards, ruined castles and forts. Maps and detailed directions are given for the route of every walk.

Joanna Young has been exploring the Skye coastline for many years and has captured her experience and discoveries in this exciting guide. Written from the perspective of an amateur walker, *Short Walks on Skye* allows ramblers of all ages and abilities to experience the pleasures of walking on this beautiful island.

50 Classic Routes on Scottish Mountains

Ralph Storer
ISBN 1 84282 091 5 PBK £6.99

Following on from *100 Best Routes on Scottish Mountains* and *50 Best Routes on Skye and Raasay*, this new volume of fifty routes, updated from the hardback edition, completes Ralph's best-selling series of guidebooks to the best of Scottish hillwalking. Like its companion volumes, *50 Classic Routes* again ranges across the Highlands to provide an outstanding cross-section of routes, from gentle hillwalks to thrilling scrambles, from popular Munros to less well-known but equally rewarding mountains that will be a revelation even to those who think they know the Highlands well.

All routes are circular, accessible by road and include a peak over 600m/2,000ft. Route descriptions are detailed yet concise, and each is accompanied by one of Ralph's famous at-a-glance route grids, which gives ratings for technical difficulty, terrain, seriousness and foul weather navigability. Maps and photographs complete the picture.

Let *50 Classic Routes* help you make the most of your days in the Highlands.

Happy walking!

Hill Walks in the Cairngorms

Ernest Cross

ISBN 1 84282 092 3 PBK £4.99

This selection of some of the most popular hill walks in the beautiful Cairngorms makes a detailed and lively companion for hillwalkers of all ages. Cross demonstrates his knowledge, love and considerable experience of walking in the Cairngorms with this varied and rewarding guide to the hills and to nearby Badenoch and Strathspey – commonly known as *Monarch of the Glen* country after being popularised by the BBC television series.

Including a step-by-step route plan for each walk, invaluable mountain safety tips and practical local advice, *Hill Walks in the Cairngorms* also makes inspiring reading for the armchair hillwalker by incorporating a comprehensive guide to the wildlife, history and surroundings of the area to make the Cairngorm landscape come alive.